Joyce Storey was born in Kingswood, near Bristol, in 1917. After leaving school at the age of 14 she worked in service for a brief period before starting a seven-year stint working in a corset factory. On the eve of the Second World War she married John Storey, an airforce man, with whom she had three daughters and a son. In 1983, at age 66, frustrated by what life seemed to offer her, Joyce joined the Bristol Broadsides writer's workshop and began her autobiography.

Joyce Storey, now retired, and partially sighted, still lives in Bristol. She has five grandchildren and a great-granddaughter, and is currently working on the third volume of her autobiography. Virago also publish *Joyce's War*, the sequel to *Our Joyce*.

Our Joyce

1917 – 1939

Joyce Storey

Her Early Years

Published by VIRAGO PRESS Limited, 1992
20–23 Mandela Street, Camden Town, London NW1 0HQ

Copyright © Joyce Storey, 1987

First published in Britain by Bristol Broadsides, 1987

A CIP catalogue record for this book is available from the British Library

Typeset by J&L Composition Ltd, Filey, North Yorkshire
Printed in Britain by Cox and Wyman Ltd, Reading, Berks

Thanks to: South West Arts, Bristol City Council, Avon County Council, Terry Eagleton, Nick Stones, Ruth Mazet, Will Gut and Ian Bild.

To Bristol Broadsides I would like to express my thanks, to Phil Smith and Norma Jaggon, also to the many friends I have made at the Southmead Group and the Women's Group at the Albany Centre. For all their support and confidence in me, their warmth and affection: without them this book may never have been written. A special thanks to Kath Horseman, who as co-ordinator in the early days, gently nudged me from the short story to the longer length autobiography. To Alana Farrell, who I first met at a writers' conference in Birmingham, who not only enthused about my work, but continued unstintingly to encourage me. Finally, my never ending gratitude to my daughter, Pat, for practical help in those dark days of deep depression after I became partially sighted. She set the pen in my hand and assured me that I could and would finish the book, making me realise that survival depends on getting up and going on again. None of this would have been possible this time without the help of my wonderful family and friends. If this narrative brings pleasure to you, dear reader, then I am most happy. I held the dream, with love and help I climbed my 'Mountain'. My life did hold purpose and meaning, the pieces did fit together. I am content. God bless you all.

Into my heart an air that kills
From yon far country blows:
What are those blue remembered hills,
What spires, what farms are those?

This is the land of lost content,
I see it shining plain,
The happy highways where I went
And cannot come again.

A. E. Housman
A Shropshire Lad

1 · *My Mother's Story*

My Mother had carried me with bitterness and resentment. Just thirteen months earlier, she had given birth to my brother Dennis, and six short months before that, she had been marched up the aisle by a tight-lipped father determined to make an honest woman of her. She recalled that it had been Harvest Festival time, and Bourne Chapel was decorated with sheaves of golden corn. In the windows stood tall pots of bronze and yellow pom-pom chrysanths. Although the sun shining through the stained glass windows was warm and touched the altar-rail where she stood, she had felt sick and cold. As she walked slowly past the shiny black pews with their red covers, her hand hardly touched her father's outstretched arm.

Philip Stacey was a big man with a big booming voice to match. That voice, plus the buckle-end of a strap was all he needed to exact obedience from his brood of six children. My Mother had often felt the strap on her unprotected legs. Even Philip's wife would run from him like a scared hare, it would never have occurred to her to do otherwise. Each night with the sound of his key in the lock, in her fresh laundered pinny, she would be ready with her hand on the big black kettle, which had been singing on the range, waiting instantly to pour the water into the china teapot. 'The master's coming,' she would say.

As she neared the altar-rail, Gilbert Charles Dark, the son of Nathaniel Dark (the local coalman), stepped forward to greet his bride, and her legs felt strangely heavy as though they were protesting at this enforced union. He had pursued her with some considerable persistence after first meeting her in the park where she had been walking with her sister Amy, and he had raised his white boater to them both. Amy had giggled, then

1

gone home to whisper to her father that the Dark boy had paid attention to 'our Nell'. After that, he had actually come calling, and always produced a red carnation from under his hat. Philip invited him to tea and asked a lot of questions. He was apprenticed as a Brass Moulder and his job so far had protected him from being conscripted for the army, but now that he was 21 he would shortly be sent to Coventry to a munitions factory. That was that, and as far as Philip was concerned, they were officially engaged. No more messing about, he wasn't having his daughter flitting from one bloke to another giving him a bad name. Nell could be a handful, a bit head-strong and high-spirited. She had an uncanny knack of looking a chap straight in the eye as though she was mocking him. A couple of babies would soon get the fancy notions out of her head; a chap knew where his wife was when she held a bairn in her arms . . .

'Who giveth this woman?' the vicar's voice was saying; and Philip's booming voice must have sounded like a death knell.

'We give our lives so glibly into another's keeping,' she once told me. It had, she said, been a quick furtive fumbling that hot July night in St. George's Park. Once again, it had been her sister who silently and slyly whispered to her father that Nell had been sick one morning when she had run all the way up Castle Street, then across Castle Ditch to the Pithay to arrive at Fry's Chocolate Factory. Amy was a foremistress in the packing department and saw her sister white and trembling, fighting uncontrollable waves of sickness. She arrived home one night, shortly after this, to find Chas, as she called him, sitting on the horse-hair sofa and her father standing by the fire.

'Well my girl,' he had said, 'It looks as though we shall have to get thee wed. Thy lad'll do the right thing by 'ee,

Joyce's Mum when young

2

and you've a house to move into — his two sisters'll let 'ee half their house up Kingswood way . . .'

And so it was that Chas brought his unwilling bride back to the house at South Road in a terrace of stone-built Victorian houses. His two spinster sisters had agreed on a rent of six shillings a week. The following April, my brother Dennis was born and the two of them, Ada and Flo, twittered with excitement and hurried from work to coo over him and carry him into the front parlour which was their domain. Chas was now in Coventry on war work and making spasmodic visits down. . . . Three months later my Mother, pregnant again, hardly noticed how frequently the baby disappeared into the other room or even heard the bolt being drawn across the door. In July of the following year, I was born and my Father made a flying visit down to see us.

He had hoped for a reconciliation between them when a little girl had been born. He loved my Mother passionately, but he couldn't express what he felt; a lack of education dammed him up, he could find no expression in words. There was no aggression in my Father and he would cry with vexation or just bite his lip and turn away. He would have done anything to please my Mother, but she never forgave him for robbing her of her precious youth. In the years that followed, she played her part as wife and mother. She cooked, she bottled and she sewed. When money was scarce, she could produce a meal from hardly anything at all; and her nimble fingers were never still. She invented things from cardboard for us kids to play with and she could paint and make paper flowers and big fat Christmas crackers. But when she met my Father's gaze, a hard look would come into those dark brown eyes of hers, as though the warmth was suddenly withdrawn and my dad would bite his lip and walk away.

I was sixteen months old when the War came to a close and an uneasy Armistice was signed. Train loads of war-scarred and battle-weary soldiers returned from France. They were to suffer one last humiliation. Not from gun-shot or blast, but from a killer 'flu virus that struck when body resistance was at its lowest and took off as many civilians and soldiers as did the war. My Father returned from Coventry with streaming eyes and a high temperature, and by the Christmas of 1918 everybody at 18 South Road was confined to bed including me.

2 · *First Impressions*

Spring brought promise of better things and Dad found work at a local foundry called Jackson's who had started up at the top of the lane. Two minutes and he could be in the yard. Mum could hand him his tucker-box and flask of tea through a hole in the corrugated sheeting that skirted the lane and hid the piles of unlovely iron moulds in the foundry yard.

Sights, sounds and sensations filled my life now, and one of my earliest memories was that of Jackson's furnace when it started up at six in the morning and hissed to a final gasp and splutter at six at night. It thumped its way through the day and shot fiery red sparks into the sky, and on washdays my Mother would shake her fist at the black monster because it would shed dirty smuts all over her clean washing. My Father brought me red sand from the foundry to play with, and made me a sand pit, and he brought my Mother's big wooden sewing machine top for me to use as a boat. But it was outside the battered old gate with its peeling paint and loose rusty lock with the spindle on the brass handle that came away in your hand that life began. We had a white collie dog called Lady and together she and I would make for the back gate and freedom. Lady had long since mastered the art of removing that handle.

She would bark and wag her tail when she saw the children.

Outside the door was a square of bare earth called The Patch, which faced the backs of the last ten houses. A lane skirted The Patch and led up and around Fry's farm, with the corrugated fence of Jackson's foundry taking up the other side of the lane. Facing the other ten houses in the terrace was a shoe factory, so we were the lucky ones, we had this half acre of dirt track to play on. The boys played football, rounders, kick-tin and marbles; and the girls ran wooden hoops, played with dolls or prams or played skipping or hopscotch. But it was The Mountain that Lady and I always made for. The Mountain was a mound of earth at the far end of The Patch piled high up against the Doctor's house. It had started off as rubble where everybody threw the stones and rubbish when the men had attempted to clear The Patch for the kids to play on, but now it was a mountain and an exciting adventure playground. I slipped and heaved and fell. I scraped my knees and hands and finally made it to the top. Several of the older boys would try to be protective and carry me to the top but I resisted all efforts of help and squirmed and wriggled away from them. My Mother would come out sometimes to drag me away from that filthy place, and I would scream until a fit of coughing stopped me from making any sound at all. The 'flu at Christmas had left me with a cough and my Mother would sometimes look at me with alarm. I followed my Father everywhere. From the Council he had rented a plot of land behind the boot factory as an allotment, and I would silently follow him there and watch every wriggling worm as it fell from his spade. I loved this silent man. He made me a seat in the hedge skirting the lane and gave me the choicest strawberries and the ripest raspberries from the line of raspberry canes that were planted along the wall of the boot factory. Then at the first stroke of tea-time, he would put me on the bar of his bike and we would ride triumphantly home.

I was three before I finally manoeuvred The Mountain. Lady would bound up ahead of me and then bark her encouragement from the top, whilst I puffed and panted and grew red in the face, completely oblivious to the stings from nettles or the stones that grazed my knees. Red clay stained my knickers when a sudden slip forced me to fall onto my rear and have to start all over again, but with Lady still barking tantalizingly from the top, I would pick myself up, rub my grubby hands on my clean dress and address Lady soberly, 'Oh dear — me fall'.

The long haul up would start again until, lobster-faced but triumphant, I would join lady at the top. I'd jump up and down with fiendish glee, with Lady barking her head off. We made such a racket that my Mother would look up from her machining, notice the gate was open, and come tearing round the corner to snatch me up and haul me inside the gate again. Thereupon, my frustration was so great, that I would jump up and down with rage and shriek with temper and again a fit of coughing would leave me pale and shaken. Sometimes it was one of the roughnecks who would take a turn at retrieving me from the top of 'that muckheap' as my Mother called it, but I'd wriggle so furiously from his grasp, that sometimes it was the both of us that took a tumble, and the lad would look apologetic and mutter, 'She ain't half got a paddy, your little 'un, Missus.'

Looking back, it must have been fairly obvious, even then, that many would try but few would succeed, in subduing me.

Despite all efforts to bar The Mountain from me, it remained a challenge and a desperate goal to win, for there was no way to explain what the view from the top revealed or did for me. I would put my arms around Lady's neck and whisper, 'Pretty trees . . . pretty flowers . . . and BOYS . . .'

Over the wall was the doctor's house right next to Fry's farm, and along the wall that divided the house from the

7

farm was a row of tall proud Cypress trees, looking like sentinels in dark green uniform. Blue delphiniums, red and pink larkspur and lupins graced the far wall. I learned all the flower names later, for my Father took a hand at growing them all in that plot of land behind the boot factory. There were green lawns and gravel paths, and then suddenly from behind a big glass conservatory two young boys would come tearing on their three-wheeler bikes. They would look up when they neared the wall and heard Lady's barking 'Hello' and wave to us, every time they came round this would be a signal for Lady's barking, and my ritual dance to start all over again.

The women from our row of ten houses would begin to sieve the ashes from their ranges all along the lane that skirted the hedge. The rain always left great pools of muddy water and attempts at trying to fill them in or breaking up the clay of this unyielding earth made the lane more unlovely Ma Saunders came out first with a green cardigan always full of holes and her long black woollen skirt covered with a coarse piece of brown sacking tied round her waist several times with black tape. Most women had their hair tied severely back, either in a bun or covered with a dust cap. Ma Saunders always wore her husband's cap. My Mother only, broke the rule; she wore a band of black velvet and her soft dark hair framed the whole of the front of her forehead and gave her a soft feminine look. Ma Saunders was always retrieving hairpins, and tiny wisps of hair escaped from beneath the brown cap that she wore. She would stare disapprovingly at Lady and me perched on top of the mound of earth and wag her finger at me, 'Stop that noise you baggage and come down from there — I'd tan yer backside if you were a lass of mine.'

Lady and I would look at each other; we both knew that she was the 'enemy' and we both knew exactly how to deal with her. As soon as she had made a few steps up The Mountain and stretched out bony hands to grab me, we would both set up such a din. I would scream right in her ear, and lady would growl and show her teeth so that Ma Saunders would stumble, fall on one knee and then beat a hasty retreat muttering, 'Temper like a racehorse that kid — I swear she's in league with the divvel.'

Meanwhile, the doctor's two boys were very interested in the rumpus that Lady and I had caused, and I'm sure they would have loved to have been allowed outside. I learned much later that their names were Aubrey and Philip, but I couldn't manage that mouthful at that early stage, so I settled for 'Bree' and 'Lillip'. Come hell or high water, I contrived with the help of Lady and all the cunning I could muster, to be there every day to gaze in awe and wonder at the garden, and to wait for that precise moment when the boys came tearing out from the bush by the conservatory.

'Br . . . um, br . . . um' they would yell and then wave, and Lady and I would go wild with excitement.

3 · *Shadow of Illness*

The roughnecks were playing football right by the doctor's surgery. We were in our usual vantage place on top of The Mountain, with Lady barking and me jumping up and down. Several people going into the surgery had glanced up in alarm as the ball screed towards them, and Mrs. Wilson from the end house had already hollered to them to 'pack it in!' Mrs. Wilson had been practising her scales (she was a singer) and she had suddenly broken off in the middle of a high note to shout through the open window. Her husband was a small man, with a face 'like a hatchet' my mother said. He kept pigeons and was whistling softly by the loft trying to get them in. When the ball hit the top of the wall and skimmed over into his yard, he suddenly made a quick

9

movement through the back gate and without any more ado began to lambast the first lad that came into his field of vision, across his head and shoulders. Sam Fry covered his battered head as best he could and staggered around like a drunken sailor. The assault continued for several minutes whilst everyone looked on in a stunned sort of silence — even Lady didn't bark. Old Hatchet Face must have exhausted himself and grown tired of meting out punishment, because he suddenly stopped the bashing and stalked back as quickly as he had shot out and resumed whistling for the pigeons-as if nothing had happened.

Poor Sam Fry, red-faced and crying, limped home up the lane yelling at the back of Mr. Wilson's head that he would get his father on to him for assault and battery. The shocked silence was broken by one of the bigger lads giving the ball a hefty kick which came straight in my direction and caught me full in the midrift, winding me so that I fell and rolled down the hill and lay on the ground gasping for breath. Fortunately, an elderly man going into the surgery had witnessed the whole thing and rushed forward to pick me up and carry me to the doctor's.

Doctor Britton was young and efficient. He first enquired from the small knot of boys crowding round the door with anxious faces, who I was and where I lived. He learned from a babble of voices all speaking at once, that I was Chas Dark's babby and a dozen grubby fingers pointed to the open yard of our house just three doors away. He dismissed them and told them they must take their ball and play in the field at the top of the lane and very sheepishly, they quietly dispersed. My Mother and Father were informed and were now ushered into the surgery white-faced with anxiety, and Dr. Britton spoke to them for a long time. Then my father picked me up and carried me over his shoulder back to the house and laid me on the hard horse-hair sofa where I cried again because the coarse horse-hair stuck into my legs, until my

Mother made a soft kapok mattress to put under me and only then did I drift off to sleep.

There had been nothing that early October Morning, to indicate that any wind of change was about to take place. I was at an age when stability was my only security, any change in the overall pattern of things I don't know how I could have coped with. Alas, I was about to find out . . .

I did not know that I was ill. The bouts of coughing did not convey a message that I was in any danger at all; or the Doctor's sudden interest in me or the talks with my Mother that left her looking worried. I doubt if the almost foreign expression 'fifty-fifty chance' that I casually heard expressed would have meant much anyway. That morning, Lady and I once more made for the gate which was already half open. She had bounded through, stopping only to bark at a wolf spider who was busy spinning a web across the top of the half open gate. As the sun shone through the web, it glistened like silver. I stopped to watch the spider weaving busily away, and I suddenly thought of my Mother and how her fingers wove the fine crochet work into a pattern as intricate as any spider's web. She was as industrious as any spider, and as clever.

Lady was bounding towards The Mountain and Ma Saunders was deep in conversation with Mr. Fry from the farm half way up the lane. A big cart with two horses was immediately behind them — a man had just thrown a shovel into the cart and was heading towards the road. When my line of vision was finally cleared, what I saw made me stop dead in my tracks. I was facing an unscalable eight foot wall of stark grey stone — The Mountain had gone. Ma Saunders' black skirt swept against me just as I was about to howl my protest to the four winds.

'That's stopped your little gallop.' She said maliciously, and disappeared into her back yard. Despondently, we gazed at the tall, bare wall. Never again would I climb to the top to see into that garden paradise, or see the familiar faces of the two boys, Lillip and Bree. Large tears rolled down my face whilst Lady sighed too and nuzzled her nose into my hand.

We walked slowly down to the surgery door. The black wrought-iron gates were closed and locked. Tonight there would be a light above the door and as I peered through the bars of the gate and even into the conservatory, there was no sound or sign of the two boys. Another wall completely obstructing the side and front of the house carried on right into South Road until you came to the big blue painted wide wooden gate which swung open to reveal another lawn with waving pampas grass and a big expanse of gravel path that swept in a wide arch right up to the front door. Right in the corner of the garden, just as you rounded the corner you had to pass under a beautiful red May tree. The scent of the blossom when it flowered in the Spring was sweet and heady. My Mother said it was sickly, but I loved it. It was not in bloom now, and as we came up to the gate I found to my unutterable joy that it was open to its fullest extent. The gardener was collecting up some rose limbs that he had been pruning, the wheelbarrow and his spade were well in evidence and I could see his little bobble cap and his white thick socks turned over his wellington boots. Without realising it, Lady and I advanced into the drive, and at that moment the two boys came tearing round the corner on their bikes, the wheels making a crunchy sound on the gravel. They pulled up slowly as they caught sight of Lady and me standing there so audaciously in the middle of their drive and shyly offered a greeting. Lady offered a paw and wagged her tail. The two boys were curious and captivated with Lady, who barked to let them know she too would love to play. I jumped up and down — it was the only way I could express the joy I felt. Hearing the rumpus, the gardener sauntered over to us and when he recognised me from the rumpus of the previous week, bent down to enquire if I was alright now. I nodded my head up and down vigorously, and he patted my head and touched my curls. At that moment, Doctor Britton strode through the gates and eyed this domestic scene with some amusement. Then he too bent down to enquire as he lightly touched my midrift: 'Does it still hurt here?'

I shook my head from side to side, then pointed to the two boys still amused with lady lifting her paw in a gesture to be friends. 'Lillip,' I said pointing, 'And Bree.'

'I see you have made the acquaintance of my two sons,' he said laughing, 'Now we must go and find your Mother, I have some news for her.'

He took my hand and I waved goodbye to the two boys. Little did I know, but it was to be some time before I would ever see them again. Events were moving swiftly now and I was to face the first upheaval of my life. At that moment though, with my hand in Doctor Britton's, I felt elated. Even the loss of The Mountain faded into insignificance at the discovery that morning of the open gates and a first-hand glimpse of that wonderful garden and the two boys excitedly Brrum, Brruming towards me on their three-wheeled bikes.

As we came into the yard, my Mother was hanging out some washing but she glanced up sharply when she saw me with the Doctor. They stood for several minutes talking in low tones and my mother looked serious and was very silent. When he had gone, she leaned against the side of the water barrel for a long time, then she sighed very deeply and once more began to hang the washing on the line.

With the November fog and fast approaching Winter, my cough grew steadily worse and there were days when I never moved from the hard, uncomfortable horse-hair sofa that became my bed. Too exhausted even to cry after one of those bouts of harsh brittle spasms of coughing, I would lie for hours just staring at the faded wallpaper with its pattern of mauve and pink flowers, and sometimes imagine I saw fairy faces and animals in the contour of the pattern. Above the sofa was a picture of Frenchay Glen in a large dutch gilt frame, and on the far wall, was a picture also in a gilt frame, of a stag with huge antlers standing proud and erect and called 'The Monarch of the Glen'. My Mother said that both paintings had been the work of a man who would offer his talents liberally to anyone who would buy him a pint. The quiet restfulness of the trees in the picture would soothe me and I could almost hear them rustle softly. I could feel the sun shining through the branches and I longed to be able to get up and go with Lady outside the battered old gate. Lady was my constant companion and would sit for hours with her head resting on the bottom of the sofa and occasionally giving a big sigh as if to say, 'When are you going to come and play?'

When Doctor Britton came, he would look very grave and once I heard him tell my Mother that it was now very serious indeed and that both my lungs were infected. She must make up her mind about something very quickly so that he could make the necessary arrangements.

Towards evening when Dad came home from work, he would come straight over to look at me and enquire what the Doctor had said. I would hold out my arms to him, but he would say coaxingly, 'Just wait for Dad to have a wash first.'

I would hear him splash about in the sink by the back door and when he came back in he would always smell of carbolic soap and his clean shirt would be a collarless striped one. Then he would pick me up and walk up and down the room with me, patting my back in a rough, kindly way that eased the pain where I had lain so long on that hard sofa. At the same time, he hummed a tune in a strange kind of trembling with his lips. I have never heard anyone else hum a tune in this way before or since. He kept up this ritual pacing, up and down, until he successfully eased me off to sleep. He was incredibly gentle and I never knew the exact moment when I came into contact with the hardness of the sofa once more.

That Winter I almost died. Of this of course I have no knowledge. Only a hazy memory of floating without effort and without pain towards the window where, although it was night-time, I thought I saw the doctor's garden with the mauve and pink delphiniums and the lupins and the larkspur and the bees buzzing from flower to flower. I was just about to drift down from the sill into the sunlit garden when I heard my Mother urgently demanding that I come back immediately.

'Come back,' she said, 'I won't let you die — Come back — Oh come back!'

I returned rather violently or so I dreamed, for it seemed that I had fallen off the sill and down onto the floor with a loud bump. Many years afterwards when my Mother related this incident about the night I almost died, these were the very words she called out to me when I had gone into a convulsion and she had called me back from the edge of death.

4 · *Painswick*

The long Winter had gone, and the birds were singing outside the bedroom window that Spring morning when I heard a sound of bustling activity from the kitchen below, and then Dad called to my Mother to hurry or we would miss the train. During the last few weeks, my cough had eased a little and my chest was not so painful, I was almost excited about the prospect of a train ride, for I had never been on one, or even on a station. My Mother carried me downstairs where the pile of new knitted garments lay ready and waiting. When the new vest was put on, I cried for it itched and irritated me, and for fear of bringing on a fresh spasm of coughing my Mother conceded to my wish and brought out a white cotton one with half sleeves. This satisfied me, and I was finally dressed in the green cape and hood, with tiny mittens to match and strapped into the pushchair that my Mother had borrowed for the occasion. Dad had packed a flask and sandwiches and, when he had checked that he had got everything, we made our way down the path to the back gate and into the lane. Lady barked at us from the sitting-room window. She couldn't understand why she couldn't come with me. felt sad because she had waited for such a long time for me to play again with her. I never saw Lady again, and my very last memory of her are those sad eyes looking at me from the window of the sitting-room. Eyes that haunt me still. The pleasure of the ride in the train blotted out my disappointment that lady could not be with us that day, for I was confident that tomorrow I would be able to tell her all about it, and then we could walk as far as the Doctor's blue gate to see if it was open once more. The lane was exceptionally muddy, and in some places Dad had to lift the pram with me in it, right over the wide wet pools. The hedges were showing little green buds, very soon now the green fresh leaves would cover them and Spring would really be here.

Of the actual journey to Painswick in the train from Warmley Station I have no recollection, or of the seriousness of the occasion. It was not uncommon for children or adults to die of tuberculosis, a disease that affected the chest and lungs, and which I had contracted with both lungs affected. Fortunately for me, Doctor Britton, who was an up-and-coming bright young doctor, was very much in favour of the new open air clinics that were just beginning to open up in England for the treatment of this complaint. Hitherto, only people who could afford to go to Switzerland returned home in health. Careful diet, exercise and rest, and plenty of good clean fresh air was the recipe, and now a few of these places had been opened up in England. (They were, they said, in the experimental stage.)

I had been chosen as a small guinea pig, along

16

with twelve other children whose ages ranged from six months to twelve years to go to an open air hospital at Painswick near Stroud. That was why my Mother had made all those woollen knitted garments and that was why I was on my way dressed in that green cape and watching all the fields rush past. But I knew nothing of that. I thought I was going for a ride.

'Hinton, Dinton, Durham, Doynton, Absom, Wick, Pucklechurch and Syston.' These were all the 'Halt' stations that a slow train would stop at and my Father could rattle them all off. Much later I would get to know and to love them for they were to be a source of endless pleasure when Dad and me would explore them on our bikes.

Right then, only a few vivid memories etched themselves indelibly on my mind. The starkest of all was the wide white gate we opened, leading up to a long white wooden bungalow with a verandah all round it. In front of the verandah were three steps leading down onto a lawn with a vegetable garden below that. At the bottom was a gate that led into a field which extended right up to the other side of the bungalow. As we walked up the path, I have a vivid memory of the big oak tree standing there like a great kindly giant. It must have been a very old tree, for several of its great branches thrust out peculiar and gnarled, deformed shapes. I grew to love this great giant of a tree. The deformed limbs made easy steps on which to climb, and when I grew well again I spent hours curled up amongst the leaves not even daring to breathe when they came calling or looking for me lest they discovered my hiding place. I told it all my secrets and in the Summer I would retire to this part of the garden to lie beneath its branches and be lulled to sleep.

A lot of parents and children were seated or standing in small knots waiting to be called into the bungalow. Matron would call a boy or girl by their Christian name first. She would take them by the hand. She had a white collar and cuffs to match. All the time I did not think it at all strange that I should be in a place like this. I thought it was all part of the lovely treat that I had been taken for a ride and now into this nice garden. It had been a long day, and I was beginning to feel very tired and ill. I wished to go home now and to go to sleep. At last, my name was called and the lady with the white collar and cuffs came out and took me by the hand and into the house.

At the end of the verandah, was a tiny little room which contained twelve little pegs from one of which hung a towel with my name on it and also on the peg was a bag with a big 'J.D.' embroidered on it and in which I recognised the brown whalebone bristle brush with which my Mother used to brush my hair every morning. I was told to take off my clothes and when I had done so, I was given a cotton vest, and then a brown cotton tunic and a pair of brown shorts. No socks, but a pair of plimsoles took the place of the brown leather shoes that I had been wearing. All the clothes that my Mother had painstakingly knitted were taken away. Years later, my Mother would relate how she had received the parcel and wept bitter tears: 'They have taken her up there to die,' she wailed in despair.

I was given a a brown wicker basket with a white disc on the front with the number fourteen on it, and was told that I must put my clothes in it every night and be responsible for it. Tea would be soon, she said. Once again, I thought that as long as my Mum and Dad were there in this house it would be alright and we would be going back tomorrow. I went in search of them and as the twilight came and the shadows lengthened, a kind of panic took hold of me. In desperation, I raced towards the gate. I saw a woman crying at the gate and giving one last anguished look back towards the house. The sound of several children sobbing from the interior of the bungalow made the terror rise in my throat almost stifling me. A nurse ran up to me, and taking my hand, turned me towards the house again.

'Your Mummy wants you to be a good girl. You are going to stay here in this nice house with us. You will like that, won't you? And you will have all these children to play with.'

I remember the room alongside the paddock and the bread and butter and jam laid on for tea. And I remember those three shudders that went through my body and the anguished, stifled sob that never came out. I had been a bad, bad girl. Those temper tantrums that everybody predicted would get me into trouble finally had. THEY had come for me at last, and now I would never see my Mother or Father again. My Mother had rejected me and didn't love me. I would have to be good from now on.

The nurse stopped for a while when she saw I wanted to say something, but no sound came. At any other time I could scream my frustration to the wind, now it seemed I could hardly breathe. I tried to get out the word 'Mummy', but all the fear and terror that I had been left in that place was trapped deep down inside me. I gave three great shudders that almost convulsed me as the nurse suddenly picked me up in alarm and carried me into that strange place and fussed over me until at last I must have slept. I never forgave my Mother.

5 · *Getting Better*

I came to love that house at Painswick. The nurses took us for walks in the countryside, and we took off our shoes, tied the laces together, and hung them around our necks and walked barefoot along the streams that babbled through the quiet lanes. We slept on the open verandah in rough army blankets tucked up snug and tight. Our beds were made up in a special way so that no matter how you wriggled the blankets stayed tight

19

around you. Only if the rain beat in or the weather was really bad, were the shutters pulled across. I grew to know and love the sounds of the night life, to hear the cry of a night owl, the bark of a vixen, and to wake in the morning to the sounds of woodpigeon and the dawn chorus of blackbirds. To hear the rustle of the wind through the trees and see the sunrise and clouds scudding across the sky. A young man would sometimes take us for long walks. He would make us run for a while, and then to fall flat on our faces and pant for several minutes. This was to expand our lungs and to learn to expel all the bad air in our lungs as well. We would roll down the hill in a grassy field, and finally we had a wonderful time collecting twigs and branches and we would make a fire and dance round it like mad dervishes.

My Mother and Father came to see me at Christmas. They sat along the side of the room in high-backed chairs and watched us from a distance whilst we tucked into jellies and cakes that the staff had made for us, all the while swinging our bare feet under the table. I kept watching them and hoping they would come to tell me that I was going home, but more than anything I wanted them to cuddle me and tell me I hadn't been a bad girl, and that they loved me and wanted me back. For some odd and obscure reason, I honestly thought that it had been because of my temper tantrums that I had been sent away to be punished. Maybe my Mother thought it best not to come to talk to me; maybe she had been told that to be upset again would undo the good progress that I was making and as it seemed I was settling down well, she had been told to watch but not communicate. I had no way of reasoning any of that out then, except to say now that I have no doubt that she must have suffered as much as I. But the feeling of suffocation arose once more when thought of being comforted and held close and she didn't come to me. When I looked up for the third time, I saw only the hard, upright chairs where they had been sitting. They had gone.

20

It seemed that my life would go on for ever in these serene and idyllic surroundings ... Kingswood, the Patch and that cold Victorian house in South Road faded from my mind and only the guilt that I had done something bad stayed like a dark silent shadow somewhere deep down inside me. From the first day when I had shuddered so violently at the disappearance of my parents I had sworn always to be good and never again to show any burst of temper so that I could go back and live with my parents again. We were escorted every morning to the schoolroom in the village where the nuns took charge of our first elementary teaching where reasoned, my punishment would be meted out. So I set to with a will to learn the tasks set before me. I learned to tie bows in record time. The cardboard clock face was harder, and I sometimes made myself sick when just a hint of impatience showed on a sister's face. I learned to be as quiet as a mouse as soon as I saw a finger raised to lips, and to stand to one side to let the next girl pass through the door at tea-time and to close the door noiselessly behind me. Even now, if I am in a 'bus queue, I will without thinking do the same thing and stand to one side to let everyone else get on before me!

But words were magic, and soon I was reading simple picture books which led me into a world where adults couldn't reach me, touch me or hurt me. And this, together with the walks and the countryside filled my soul with a joy and a peace I could not describe. So whilst my body filled out and rounded, and my face took on a healthy hue, I also became a silent, solitary child who found more pleasure in playing alone than with others, except that I was not alone. I heard voices in the wind, felt the sun warm on my back and when I ran through the tall grass or picked the yellow cowslips I would suddenly cry out loud:

'I love. I love. I love!'

The days and months passed, each one very much like another and I found a kind of stability in their sameness,

I began to feel secure in the constancy. In the playroom, I had found a battered celluloid doll with a bashed nose and cracked face. I adopted it and carted it everywhere. It resembled a boy doll and, because it was warm to the touch and not cold like a china doll, I would cuddle it and kiss it and hold it close to me. I talked to it for hours and together we would hide away in my secret place in the tree.

There came a day when something different did happen. I had just reached the classroom when one of the nuns, with a swish of her habit, bade me follow her and when I was facing her she told me that I had been a good girl and that now I was better I would be going home again. My Father would be coming to fetch me back the next morning. I was now five and a half years old and had been away from home for eighteen months.

There were so many things I had to do. Say goodbye to Maisie the horse who so often had ambled up to the window of the dining hall and where I would feed her all the crusts I so hated eating on my bread; take off my shoes and wade in the stream that ran along the bottom of the paddock. Most of all I wanted to wrap up my boy doll. Someone had told me that we couldn't take any of our toys out of the home because it was a fever hospital and wasn't allowed, but I had sneaked a large piece of brown paper and I thought that if I wrapped up my doll in a parcel and took it out hidden in my clothes, nobody would be any the wiser, so I remember sitting on the verandah and trying to wrap up this boy doll.

Then a shadow fell across the step and I saw my Father with his blue eyes, smiling down at me, but looking slightly embarrassed at the obvious change in me as though I was a strange new person he hadn't seen before. Then I stood up and said I hoped he wasn't too tired from his journey and that I was all ready if he wished to go. I have a hazy recollection of walking a long way to the station and passing under an archway — which must have been in Stroud. The only memory of the journey is

22

the indescribable loss of my boy doll and the sudden knowledge that they must have snatched it at a time when I was preoccupied. The treachery was too much to bear but I dare not cry because I had promised to be good and this would complicate things still further. As we approached Warmley Station my Father suddenly repeated the names of the local stations we were passing: Hinton, Dinton, Durham and Doynton, Absom, Wick, Pucklechurch and Syston.

My Mother was at the station to meet us. So was Aunt Flo and Aunt Ada and my brother Dennis in a new white sailor suit and hat and white doeskin boots. He immediately turned his back on me and hid his head in Aunt Ada's skirt. Aunt Flo said,

'Haven't you grown into a big girl, Joyce?'

Ada said,

'You'm like a farmer's wench.'

My Mother looked at me for a long time but didn't say a word and I remember that my Father went towards her but she turned away and then he hustled us all out of the station and we walked slowly home up that familiar Warmley Hill past The Tennis Court Hotel and up to the tram terminus. We walked past the Church, and the clocktower and into Regent Street, past the Regent Cinema, and the sweet shop and garage next door, then round the corner to South Road with Moons the Ironmongers on the corner, owned and run by two odd little spinster sisters and so home to that cold Victorian house that even now, like a dark shadow beckons, with its unhappy memories still sharp and crystal clear.

My Mother took me upstairs to show me the back bedroom that had been freshly whitewashed for me and the medicated smell that had been left behind reminded me of the Infirmary. An iron hospital bed and a chest of drawers were the only furniture, but a corner wardrobe and the curtains at the window made a gay contrast in chintz with large roses in the pattern and my Mother had made a colourful patchwork quilt for the bed. On the bed was a new china doll that had been dressed by my Mother, but I hardly looked at it for remembered the warm celluloid boy doll that I had left at the home and once more I struggled with emotions that were made the harder by having to repress them.

Our big kitchen had a shiny black range and my Father had made up the fire and had laid the cloth for tea. Dennis was nowhere to be seen and had disappeared into the front room with the two Aunts. I sat at the table with a huge piece of cake in front of me and a breakfast cup full of tea. I waited for 'Grace' to be said and my Mother smirked when I asked her if I should say it.

'You can forget that rubbish,' she said, 'You're home now.'

'Would you please pass the bread and butter?' I am reputed to have said and my Mother laughed and said to my Father:

'We have a proper bloody lady here.'

I enquired after Lady and was told that she had been destroyed. I felt desolation that was almost unbearable. I felt as though Lady was waiting for me to open the gate and the both of us would explore the waiting world beyond the gate together. The Patch was empty and I suddenly wanted the familiar surroundings: the wide open verandah where you could lie snug and warm and hear the hoot of an owl or the cry of a vixen and smell the smoke from a woodfire and the wild honeysuckle, see the clouds racing across the sky or the moon riding amongst the bright stars and then wake on a cold and frosty morning and run across the frozen blades of grass and see the spiders' webs in the hedges. That night as I lay in that cold back room, I looked out onto a bare blank wall and cried to go home.

'I want to go home,' I howled softly into the bed-clothes so that they wouldn't hear me, 'I want to go home.'

6 · *Schooldays*

In the days that followed, I went to school. Two Mile Hill School was an elementary school for working class children and stood on the top of a hill that loped all the way down to St. George and was two miles long. I had been used to a quiet little class of about half-a-dozen children with at least three sisters wending to and fro. Conversation was subdued and a loud giggle was instantly suppressed when a finger was pressed to the lips, but it also meant that we sometimes had a whole period of individual attention. Now it was noisy activity with little boys showing natural aggression and taking coveted possessions away from other children — a vast expanse of playground where the children divided; the boys played their boisterous games and the girls found quiet corners to play skipping and pottle or to bring brightly coloured wool and knot holey and uneven lengths of knitting. I hated the noise and confusion. Even the whistle blowing disturbed me, and although it taught me at the first sound immediately to get into line, I have never lost the desire to throttle the person who dares to desecrate the peace, and to regiment and condition young minds. I rebelled then as I do now, and the dark thoughts that lay smouldering beneath belied the bland expression as I promptly got up and filed into the classroom with the others.

Every morning on our way to school, we stopped at the top of the lane to watch Tom Pillinger making the sparks fly off the anvil as he shoed the lovely shire horses at the forge. The chink of hammer on steel and the hiss of the steam when the shoe was plunged into water, we stood and watched in rapt silence fascinated, and unable to move until the faint sound of the bell galvanised us into action.

Every Friday I was excused school because I had to

attend the clinic at Warmley. We would have to walk the three miles down and back in order to obtain a free jar of Cod Liver Oil and Malt plus a glass of free milk three times a week at school. I loved the Cod Liver Oil and Malt and would often rush in from play to take a spoon and dip it into the jar to savour the treacly stuff. We had a big pantry under the stairs and all kinds of delicious smells emanated from there. Mum would make wine and there were always delightful mysterious things happening inside the big stone jar where the wine was fermenting. Sometimes when it had been bottled and corked, we would suddenly hear a loud bang and the cork would fly out from the bottle and all the wine would dribble down the sides like coloured froth. We would often come in from play and take a great swig from a bottle of elderberry or gooseberry or dandelion wine, then cut a huge chunk of crumbly Cheddar cheese. Other favourites of mine were Nestles condensed milk on bread, and Lyles golden syrup and pork dripping on toast. We made toast on the big range holding the bread close to the fire on the prongs of a long toasting fork.

The roughnecks from The Patch had all crowded round that first morning I had opened the gate, and were all agog to find out how Chas Dark's little 'un had fared after that long spell away. They had heard from their parents that I'd only had a fifty-fifty chance and no doubt they were all familiar with the outcome of this dreaded illness for the cure was only in its infancy and poverty and poor conditions still contributed a great deal to its many victims.

'How bist thee?'

They had all fallen silent when I had replied in beautiful clipped English, 'Very well, thank you.'

One had giggled and with an exaggerated gesture exploded with laughter and said with mock derision, 'I say, I simply must ask Pater if I can speak to you.'

Then they all drifted away and I was left feeling very isolated and lonely. But later on I learned to play Kick

Tin and Rounders and every Saturday a whole gang of us walked to the woods. We found our own den and I learned to swing on the rope, to go exploring and make a camp fire, and become one of the lads.

On Sunday, I went to Sunday School and every Sunday afternoon my Mother would meet me and we would walk again the two miles to St. George to have tea with Gran and Granfer. All the family would be there and we would all sit round a big wooden table and have seedy cake and prunes for tea. My Grandfather was a big man of six foot with a moustache and a shock of baby fine white hair. He would sit in a big wooden chair by the fire and recount stories of murders that were published in a long thick paper called 'Thompson's Weekly News.' Nobody dared interrupt him, and all us children had to stay as quiet as mice. We were not allowed in the parlour, that was a room which stayed musty with disuse and a big aspidistra always blotted out the light from the window and prevented anyone from looking in. Gran always sat in a chair the other side of the fire and fanned herself with her apron. She suffered from 'hot blooms' — a condition my Grandfather said was peculiar to women. By the way he hollered and shouted I would have staked my life her condition was entirely due to him. He had a way of completely dominating her so that if and when she spoke at all, it was in a timid and frightened way, and if she didn't move at his first quiet demand, he would raise his voice to a yell and she would almost run to do his bidding. I hated my Grandfather with a hatred I was almost afraid to think about, and he viewed me with the same dislike and distrust that he held for my Father.

'Chas Dark has no spine,' he announced to all and sundry. 'And our Nell's so wild and headstrong she needs a heavy hand. She's too strong a personality for Chas and he'll rue the day.'

My Father would sit tight-lipped and silent in front of the whole family who never said a word. One day Grandfer took some watercress from a plate and

27

suddenly flicked the water at everybody sitting round the table, slapping his sides and roaring with laughter. I jumped along with everybody else, but hadn't been amused, 'I didn't find that at all funny.' I announced.

Grandfer's face went a pale shade of purple and he roared loud enough to make everyone tremble and look uncomfortable. He fixed watery blue eyes on me and exploded, 'And what, young Madam, would you find amusing?'

'I would like it, Grandfer, for you to shout less at Grandma and the rest of us.'

My Mother smirked, for she had no love for her Father and she had often felt the buckle end of a strap across her legs. She had a champion, now, in me. My Father had suffered insults enough and he was right there now to defend this innocent but unfortunate remark. But Philip was already turning angrily to his daughter and son-in-law.

'You are not a man at all if you can't control the wilfullness of your daughter nor the wildness of your own wife. The young 'un will land up on the front page of The News of The World and our Nell will lead you such a dance, you'll not know if you're on yer ass or yer 'ead.'

Gran's face had gone turkey red and she was fanning herself vigorously with the end of her apron. The rest of the family got up to go but Philip's booming voice demanded that they stay. So we all glared at one another until Auntie May said in her calm tones that she thought things had gone far enough and that she and Alfie, her husband, wanted to get ready for Chapel and as they were in the choir they would have to be excused. I began to think that, as far as Philip and Ellen, my grandparents, were concerned, I was still as bad as ever and that nobody would ever love me enough to hold me close and tell me I was good. Even my Mother was bad and wicked, and although I felt guilty at thinking this, she had sent me away and I thought of all those nights when I had cried silently into the pillow and had finally decided that nobody must ever know. My Mother must have thought, too, of the nights she had lain awake and cried for me, but she never told me for she kept her feelings shut away and locked so the moment was lost and gone forever and the distance began to grow further between us.

Sometimes when the family enmity abated somewhat, we would have enjoyable family evenings and Grandfer would play the organ and we would all sing those lovely Sankey hymns like 'We shall meet, but we shall miss him, there will be a vacant chair' or

'Have you had a kindness shown?
Pass it on.
'Twas not given for you alone,
Pass it on.
Let it travel down the years,
Let it wipe another's tears,
'Till in heaven the deed appears,
Pass it on.'

Alfie and May had good voices and they could sing and make us all join in. Auntie May lived in rooms across the street. Hardly anybody in those days could afford a house and the rent for rooms ranged from four shillings (20 pence) to six shillings (30 pence) a week. Perce, who was the youngest of my Mother's brothers, wanted to be wed and was demanding that Philip open up the front room for him and Glad. He would have his own way too, my Mother said . . .

Every Whit Monday there was a trip up the river in a barge. This was the event of the year and Philip would play his silver-ended squeeze-box and we would all sing 'We are out on the ocean sailing to our home beyond the sea.' We would sail right up to Bee's Tea Gardens and all the kids had a wonderful time playing hide-and-seek and going down to the river's edge where we could watch the rush of water tumbling over the weir. The sun would be warm and there would be masses of bluebells in the woods and young lovers would walk hand in hand along the river bank, and we would be given pennies by uncles we hadn't seen for ages and parents would suddenly become reckless with hard-earned cash and we would be given an unexpected ice-cream or a glass of lemonade.

Whitsuntide was an exciting week when all the Sunday Schools marched with banners flying and bands playing. The traffic was halted and the crowds at Kingswood and all the way down Two Mile Hill deep indeed. You had to be up early in the morning to get in front to see every-thing that went by. Before I started to go to Zion Chapel, I used to dance in front of the man with the big drum. On a hot day he would have to mop his face with a red handkerchief, the perspiration would run down his face and then down his nose and drop onto his drum but I just kept on dancing, that is, until one year my Mother caught sight of me in the procession and darted in and dragged me out.

'Showing yerself up like that,' she would say.

But I had loved the wild abandon; it was like the freedom of the fields, giving yourself up to the music and the beat of the drum. It seemed that all the things I loved to do were bad and wicked and any day I would be sent back again. Then I thought to myself that it hadn't been so bad and wicked to do those things there, they had encouraged you to be wild and free. It seemed that it was only when other people were around that you suddenly had to behave in an unnatural way, and being honest, and saying what you thought always upset somebody, even if you were polite. Growing up was not easy. Nor trying to please them.

When all the Sunday Schools had marched down as far as the Worlds End pub at St. George, they turned there and came back to Soundwell Road at Kingswood. G. B. Britton was a shoe manufacturer and owned a big house at Lodge Causeway. Outside the gate was a man with a big basket of buns and we all had a bun and some fruit and nuts, then we were allowed into the garden of Mr. G. B. Britton and his garden was like fairyland with rose

30

gardens and bowers and unusual tropical trees. I loved the garden and spent the entire time in a world of my own talking to imaginary people and to the trees and flowers. It was in a quiet corner of the garden that I met Mr. Britton. He came upon me holding a conversation with a non-existent person and with considerable politeness and trying to hide his own amusement, apologised for interrupting us!

At that time, I had the most beautiful hair that fell to my waist in six complete ringlets and was the colour of burnished gold. Every morning my Mother brushed it with a whale-bone brush until my scalp tingled, and my hair covered my shoulders in glorious waves. When everyone else had to put their hair into rags or pipe cleaners to make it curl, mine was a sea of natural waves and colour. By the time I came home at lunchtime, my hair had developed a character all of its own and had transformed itself into six complete fat perfect curls. Even when you inserted a finger right through the tip of the ringlet, you could not disturb its splendour and my Mother would tie the whole six curls with a coloured ribbon every afternoon. I was at an age when my hair was not a feature I ever thought about, but plenty of people commented on it and would touch the curls. G. B. positively glowed and patted my head and waxed enthusiastic about its virtues. Then he presented me with a white peace rose and told me that his wife adored roses and that all the roses in the garden were hers. When I think of G. B. I remember the white rose and how he spoke about his wife and her love of roses and on the spur of the moment I asked him if I could come and sit in his garden again, and he said quietly that I could come anytime I liked.

7 · *The Lilac*

The Lilac, a deep, deep mauve, hung in glorious profusion over the wall that divided my Grandparents' garden from the house next door. The tree belonged to Ma Parsons, and had never been trimmed back. Now, after a sudden May shower, it hung heavily scented and beautiful, in glorious confusion everywhere.

The more I gazed at it, the more convinced I became, that Gran would love to have some for her sideboard, or in the centre of the square deal kitchen table that stood in the kitchen. Back home, there were jars of flowers everywhere, even on the windowsills. Bright yellow buttercups, cowslips and bluebells, and soon there would be big white moondaisies that we would bring in from the meadows and woods. Here there was nothing except the dark green leafed Apidistra that stood on the small table in the bay window of the front room.

I was already snapping and tearing at the heavy-laden limbs of the lilac, when I saw out of the corner of my eye my Grandfather bearing down on me, his face livid with rage. I was used to my Grandfer bellowing and shouting, but unlike my Grandmother who ran to do his bidding like a scared rabbit, I merely waited for him to come up to me.

'And who, may I ask, gave you permission to pick the lilac?' he said in a voice like thunder. 'The bush belongs to Mrs. Parsons next door and is her property.'

'It's over your side of the wall.' I said simply.

Now, absolutely purple with rage, he snatched the blooms away from me and marched me through the hallway and into Ma Parsons next door.

Ma Parsons was a tall, skinny woman. She now emerged from the interior of the back kitchen holding a dirty tea-towel in her hand. She was attempting to dry a black saucepan that was so ingrained with grease and grime on the outside, that it was making the tea-towel even dirtier with each wipe she made. She peered enquiringly at the pair of us as we advanced towards her, and blinked with small watery blue eyes. Stopping her cleaning for a second, she said,

'Well . . .?'

She wore a black skirt pulled across her waist and secured with a large safety pin, her blue cardigan was faded and rolled up at the elbow. There was a gaping hole on the shoulder and this had been loosely drawn together with a different shade of wool.

'This THIEF,' and Grandfer emphasised the word, 'Has taken it upon herself to pick your lilac. If she were a wench of mine, I'd take a strap to her. Just wait 'til our Nell come in tonight to fetch her, I shall have a few words to say to her about the liberties this girl takes.'

Ma Parsons stared back blankly, but taking the lilac that was thrust at her, she threw the greasy tea-towel into a corner of the kitchen and pressed her nose into the perfume blooms and muttered 'Oh'.

'Apologise!' bellowed Grandfer shaking me until my head began to rock from side to side, 'Just say you are sorry — you little THIEF.' 'I am not a thief,' I shouted back at him, 'And don't you dare touch me!'

Shaking myself free of him, I turned and fled, leaving both of them staring back at me, one in a blind mad rage, and the other with a look of utter surprise in her watery eyes.

I ran out into the street. At the top was Avonvale Cemetery. I ran like the wind through the gateway and hid behind a big tombstone until my anger and fright had subsided. When I was quite sure that nobody had followed me, I began to play quite happily among the gravestones. I imagined that all the dead people were being held captive under the ground. I would go up to the grave and say dramatically,

'Take my hand and I will set you free,'

Then I saw the gravedigger leaning on his shovel and

looking at me. When he began to shout 'Get yerself off home!' I ran in the opposite direction so that he couldn't see me.

From a grass verge, below the vale was the river snaking its way along the Netham and skirted by woods either side. It would be soon be Whitsun when we would all be going up the river again. I began to think about Whit Monday and its coming delights and I curled up on the bank and went to sleep. When I opened my eyes, it was cold and I was hungry. I wondered if my Mother had arrived to fetch me back, for she had dropped me at Grans' that morning before going to the clinic with our Dennis. I wondered if I should venture back now. I saw the gravedigger glancing my way and I scooted out of a side turning and into the street. As I tiptoed along the passage, I heard Grandfer still bellowing and telling my Mother the tale. I peeped through the crack in the door and saw Gran fanning herself with the end of her pinny. His loud voice must have brought on one of her hot blooms. Denny was sitting on a stool in front of the range, they must have yanked out some of his teeth because he was holding a big piece of cotton wool to his mouth. He looked fed up and miserable.

'I tell 'ee, Nell, yo'me goin' to have trouble with that girl if you don't curb the high spirits of ern. I only tell 'ee fer yer own good. Spare the rod and spoil the child.'

'Knock one devil out and let half a dozen in,' said my Mother, 'I can't say the strap ever done a lot fer me.'

Grandfer began to spit and splutter.

'I didn't spare the rod and I ken hold me head up with all the buggers down the street.'

'You might be able to hold your head up, but I couldn't sit down fer days!' retorted my Mother, 'neither did I forget it or think it did me much good.'

He was staring at her now, unable to believe that she was standing up to him. I slipped in quietly and stood by her side.

'Besides,' she went on, 'What was so wrong in our Joyce

34

picking a bit of lilac? And over your side of the wall an'
all, it's yours to pick if you've a mind to. Old nose bag will
have a field day with the story you've made up to tell her.
Haven't you any thought for me without filling her
mouth with gossip?'

To my utter amazement, my Grandfather's face began
to crumple and he actually began to whine.

'I never meant no 'arm, Nell,' he snivelled, 'I only
wanted to point out to 'ee what a headstrong wench your
Joyce is. If she ain't curbed now, she'll land up on the
front page of The News of The World.'

'You call her headstrong because she has a bit of spirit
and that is what you want to thrash out of her like you tried
to thrash out of me and all your kids. Well,' and she leaned
towards him as she spat out the words, 'Well, let me tell you
something. She has something of my spirit and I glory in
it, and neither I nor her father will raise one finger to
beat that out of her like you tried to beat it out of us.'

Looking very grim and triumphant, she stood up to
depart. Instinctively both Denny and I moved to her side,
Denny with the wad of cotton wool still pressed to his
mouth looking very white and sick. When she got to the
door she again turned on her Father. 'And don't go
taking out yer nasty temper on our Mother,' she hissed
at him, 'Or you'll have me to reckon with.' She pushed
her face right into his then and said, 'And no more
remarks about Chas not being man enough to keep his
wife in order, for I've been the butt of your vile jokes
for long enough. You threw me at this man, so don't
undermine our marriage now.'

Grandfer was actually scared now, and I saw his small
beady eyes fill with tears. He looked pathetic as he stood
in the doorway and saw us go.

The rain that had threatened all day now began to fall
in big fat drops. We hardly heard him call to us from the
doorway, 'Bide a bit, Nell, till the rain goes off.'

We had already turned the corner and were heading
for the long trek home.

8 · *Ada and Flo*

I hardly ever saw my brother Dennis. He was locked away somewhere in that silent front room. Sometimes on a Sunday I would knock softly on the door and ask to be allowed in, and they would let me.

There were several things in that front parlour that I loved to stand and look at. One was the blood-red epergne which occasionally had carnations or roses in it and looked very grand and regal. It gave the room an air of great splendour, an elegance that belonged to the gentry who lived in mansions just like the ones you saw in magazines. The other was a wondrous thing full of magic that filled me with excitement so that my eyes shone. It would have been worth throwing a tantrum to be allowed into that room just to see it. To the left of the fire breast was a gas jet complete with a gas mantle. When the gas was turned on in the evening, the whole room was bathed in a soft yellow light. In order to obtain this light, pennies had to be fed into a red metal box which was behind the front door in the passage outside. My Mother would contribute two pennies and the two Aunts the other two, carefully placing them on the mantelshelf until they were needed. Four pennies would take you up to ten o'clock when the gas would run out and leave you in darkness until you inserted more money into the meter, but nobody would ever extend the lighting after ten o'clock. After that it was either candles, or a big oil lamp that would have to be lit. Round Aunt Ada's gas mantle was a gas shade made of long crystal glass drops that caught the light and danced like a thousand tiny stars, and when they were ever so lightly touched they jingled like fairy music from a magic sphere. I weaved a thousand dreams from just one touch until I was brought back to cold reality by Aunt Ada boxing my ears and telling me,

Dennis on his kettle drum

'Leave the bloody thing alone, or is that something else
you want to destroy? You don't see our Denny fingering
things and wanting always to break them.'

It had been to this room that they had brought 'our
Denny' when he had been six months old, when my
Mother found herself pregnant a second time and had

been devastated by the discovery. She hadn't minded the two Aunts twittering over him and caring for him. According to my Mother, Mother Love was not instinctive, and just because nature decrees you can have a child doesn't mean that it can make you love it. In the years that followed my birth and the resulting health problems she had with me, she must have been glad of the help and care Ada and Flo lavished upon the boy, and they certainly took care of his every need. They waited on him hand and foot and when they took him for walks or wheeled him in the pram, they told everyone that he was their boy and that he was a son sent from the good Lord to them.

This state of affairs existed only until I returned from Painswick when a single voyage of discovery led me to the front parlour and the knowledge that there was another child to play with behind the locked door. It seemed now that I was the cause of a general disruption in the usually quiet running of the house. My faint tapping on the door would for the most times be ignored and I would have to walk disconsolately away. Sometimes Aunt Ada's hard brittle voice shooing me away would send me back to the corner in the kitchen where I would sit on the box fender and look out at the dark blank wall.

Sometimes though, Aunt Flo, who was the gentlest of the two (and I could often get round her) would allow me to come and sit round the fire with them and Dennis would let me read his last week's comic. Aunt Ada would sometimes read it to us in a flat, expressionless voice and then we would have a fit of the giggles and be falling about helpless with laughter. It nearly always ended up with me being shoved outside the room again and the bolt drawn across the door.

When we went to school, I would go out the back way and Dennis through the front. If we walked home together, I would stop only long enough to see Ada let him in, and then I would run round to the back and let myself in that way. In the end, it led to trouble and I, of course, was the root cause of it. Dennis was a non-aggressive boy and in the main I liked being with him. He shared his books and his toys with me and had a sense of humour that made me laugh and giggle. He had expensive toys that the two Aunts bought him and would keep hidden until I was safely out of the way, but it was a simple John Bull printing outfit that was the cause of all the trouble. You simply put little character letters with a pair of tweezers into a wooden margin, then pressed the completed sentence on to an ink pad and then on to a piece of white paper. Hey presto! you could make up your own magazine. We had already experimented with our thumb prints and the whole of our palms, and the tablecloth — all starched and stiff and pristine white — seemed too inviting and appropriate to miss out on, so I pressed a perfect imprint onto the tablecloth.

Denny sensed danger before I did, and just as a perfect pair of palm prints appeared on the cloth a shadow fell over us and a long bony hand thumped me on the back. Dear Denny whined,

'Our Joyce did it. She made me do it.'

'I'm going to get the Black Maria to take you away — they will put you in a straight-jacket — there's no end to your wickedness.'

All this and more from Aunt Ada, but it was the thought of the Black Maria that filled my soul with such dread that I began to sob uncontrollably and to kick and scream at the thought of being taken away forcibly and put into a straight-jacket where I might never be able to struggle free. Both my Mother and Father rushed into the room and I tried to tell my Mother between sobs that I had only wanted to play with the printing set. My Father took me from the room but my Mother stayed to have a battle of words with the two Aunts stating emphatically that that was that and Dennis should now come out into his own room where no more favouritism could take place, and no more toys bought that we could fight over. With that, Ada started to wail,

39

'Don't take my baby away from me.'

'Don't talk so wet — he's not your baby.'

Ada walked out into the street and began to shout, 'She's taking my boy away from me.'

My Father ran out after her whilst Flo, pointing a finger at my Mother, said quietly but viciously,

'If anything happens to our Ada I'll wipe the floor with you.'

Then they both held on to my brother's shoulders as my Mother tried to drag him from the room. Mother said with sudden fury, 'He shall come out with us and I will get him away from you two mad buggers.'

And she and Dad began to pull at his legs, with Ada and Flo tugging at his arms and shoulders whilst Denny boy just lay supine there, not turning a hair or twitching a muscle. All this time, I was twisting my handkerchief round and round until it was a tight soggy length. What had happened was all my fault and as I watched the tussle felt bad, and wished I could stop the loud beating of my heart. My Mother suddenly let go of my brother's feet with a disgusted 'What's the use?' and left the room with my Father following her saying, 'Don't get yerself upset, Nell my love.'

She gave him a withering and half-disgusted look, 'You're a spineless bastard, anyway.'

Dad was silent and bit his lip. It was a terrible stigma in those days to be told you had no father so he walked past her and out into the back where my Mother said he would go into a king-sized sulk, and not speak for weeks which suited her just fine. Then she caught sight of me and told me to stop snivelling and get to bed, nobody was going to put me in a straight-jacket and I must learn not to be so touchy. I fled up the stairs and into that cold and white-washed room.

It was peaceful the next day and my Mother was making cakes and small buns. I asked her if I could lick out the bowl when she had finished but she said to get on with what I was doing and leave her alone in peace.

The cake smelt delicious when it came out of the oven and she placed it on the dresser with a tea-towel covering it. Ada emerged from the parlour with two blue tea-plates in her hand; could she have just a couple of slices 'Fer our Denny?' No answer from my Mother, but she indicated that she could. Ada wielded the knife with a flourish and cut two huge chunks which rendered the cake to half size, and then proceeded to scrape up the crumbs between her forefinger and thumb and stuff them into her mouth.

'My God,' exploded my Mother, 'Why don't you take the bloody lot?'

Ada, now with a slight satanic gleam in her large, heavily-lidded eyes, turned on her accusingly,

'You begrudge yer own child a farthingsworth of cake!'

And as if to emphasize the point, she held up a little finger and spat out,

'A fardon'worth!'

Two minutes later Flo trotted out and dragged her sister back to the front parlour with my Mother shouting after her,

'What about the other half for next week?'

My Dad, coming from the garden, enquired what all the shouting was about and Mum, with a scornful sigh, and mock derision replied,

'Those two harpies have got loose again.'

9 · Brother Cliff

I was nine when my brother Clifford was born on a cold November day, with the snow falling so thick and fast that you couldn't see through the flakes of snow as thick as half-crowns. My Mother, dispirited and weary, had carried this baby with the same unwillingness that she had carried me and my brother, except this time she had been violently sick and ill all the way through. My Father had been put on short time at Jackson's; three days on and three days off, which meant that he could not sign on the dole Dad would bring vegetables from the garden in the summer but there was not much to dig up in winter. Although coke was only a shilling a bag, from twelve shillings a week and six of that to go on rent, it meant times were very hard and sometimes there just was no coke to heat the house. We had very little meat, but you could get a pennyworth of bones from the butcher and Mum would put them in the oven by the side of the range with baked jacket potatoes and we would tuck into the bones and tear at the strips of meat that still hung in delicious fatty layers on them. Pork trotters were another delightful and satisfying repast. Brought piping hot from the boiling water, we could gnaw happily away at them and use the liquor for stew the next day. Most of the time we existed on bread and dripping, but there were a lot of others in the same boat and clothes and furniture were pawned to buy essentials.

I well remember that cold Victorian house where in winter great gusts of icy wind would sweep along the cold stone passageway through gaps under the front door making the frail frame of the door rattle and shake as though the draught and wind were struggling to gain entrance into the very room itself. I have images of my Father padding along the lino-covered floor, the candle that he held in the blue chipped enamel holder making weird patterns on the wall. The hiss of the unlighted gas jet, and the sudden burst of yellow flames would fascinate and soothe me as I lay scared and terrified in my iron bed, for the sudden draught from the door would make the writhings of the unmantled jet assume the wild gyrations of some exotic eastern belly dancer. Sometimes I could almost hear the thin high notes of a reed pipe played by a scarlet-turbaned Hindu sitting cross-legged on a straw coloured mat with an uncoiled cobra swaying to and fro, both suspended momentarily in one unholy truce.

When the windows rattled, we would shove little wooden wedges between the corded panes and even thick faded blue curtains hung on a fat round pole were not enough to stop the cold or the draught from seeping through. At night-time it was just as though unseen hands were shaking them from behind. You sat in front of the fire with your face and hands and knees aglow whilst your back froze. Most of the house was lino-covered with peg mats we all pegged from cut-up bits of material and on frosty days the windows would be iced up and you shivered when you had to get out of bed and go down over the stairs.

This morning there had been no fire to come down to and the snow had piled up against the back door in a high drift and some had actually blown under the back door and into the scullery. Dad had given me a hot cup of tea and told me to be quiet and good. He said that my Mother was not very well and he was going to get some coke and half a pound of biscuits for her.

I heard him in the yard shovelling the snow away from the back door and down the back path and then he pulled out the hand cart and put on his trilby and scarf. I heard my Mother shout out as if in pain and rushed up the stairs to find her stretched across the bed clutching at the bedclothes and shaking with cold and pain so that the bed was jerking up and down.

'Go and fetch Elsie Storey,' she panted, 'And tell her to come quick, the baby is coming.'

I raced over the road and knocked loudly on the knocker, yanking it up and down until my wrist hurt. Bert Storey, Elsie's husband, came slowly to the door. He still had a napkin tucked into the neck of his shirt and had been tucking into bacon and eggs.

'Hello, Joyce,' he said, 'Is there anything wrong?'

I jumped up and down on the step.

'My Mummy is dying,' I said simply, 'And she says the baby is coming.'

'Oh dear, I'll fetch Elsie,' he said.

I was told to stay with Bert until she returned and went into a house so vastly different from ours, that I stood in the kitchen with my mouth wide open.

The design of the house was the same but from the moment you stepped through the front door you felt a softness under your feet and you almost sank into thick pile carpets that seemed like heaven to walk on, and as I passed through the middle room on my way to the kitchen, the warmth from a coke fire, red hot and piled high, made me take a deep breath and sink into a big brown velvet chair beside it and stretch out my hands to warm them. Bert began again to tackle his breakfast, eating with quick bird-like motions, first cutting a piece of bacon, then egg, then fried bread. This he would stuff into his mouth and wash down with a swig of tea. Then the whole process would be repeated very quickly as though he was anxious to finish it in case someone came and snatched it away. He looked up and saw me looking at the contents of his plate, disappearing so rapidly whilst I was busy watching. He suddenly finished the whole lot and then with his knife he scraped the remaining bits of egg from the plate and licked them into his mouth, and then he actually licked the plate clean across several times with his tongue. Still looking at me he leaned over to the plate that Elsie had left, and slapped the bacon and egg between two slices of bread and handed it to me on a plate.

'Tuck in,' he said, 'I shall make some more tea.'

Never had anything tasted so delicious and by the time I had finished, grease and egg had dribbled down my chin and the heat from the fire had burnt my legs so that I had to move back. I had another cup of tea before we heard Elsie returning and she swept into the kitchen closely followed by my Father.

Outside the kitchen window on the tiny dirt patch between the wall of the next house was a mountain of coke. The blank wall had been painted white which made

44

it a bright spot to look out on, and made the kitchen lighter as well, but the pile of coke must have covered four or five feet of the wall. As I'd come through the house, had noticed another fire in the other room and one more thing noticed as well, and that was the flowers. Huge gold and bronze chrysanthemums arranged beautifully in tall vases, and curtains with deep pelmets and sashes to hold them back. God, this house was beautiful! I made a sudden and silent vow that one day I would have a house with carpets and red velvet curtains. Elsie had made this deep impression on me and although I didn't know it then, my life was to be inextricably bound up with hers.

She proceeded to tell my Father that he was to help himself to the coke and to light a fire in the bedroom for my Mother. She called the boy from next door to tell him to go at once and try to contact the nurses who lived at the Nurses' Home in Hanham Road and to tell them it was urgent and that they must come at once. It was still snowing and the lad grumbled, but he put on an oilskin and went trudging up the road, not very quickly because the great white flakes still fell silent and heavy and covered everything in a thick carpet of snow which piled in great drifts and made visibility almost nil.

The rest of that day was a memory of hectic comings and goings. At ten past twelve my Mother gave birth to a little boy. He was not a full-term baby, they said, he was a 'seven-month' baby who would need a lot of attention. Elsie kept my Mother in hot drinks and soup and kept me informed about all that was happening but she would not let me go to my Mother. She said I would only be in the way. She came over once and then I heard her pulling out drawers upstairs. When she came down, she held a shawl and several items of baby wear in her arms. She explained that the baby had come so quickly that Mum had not had time to buy it any clothes, but I knew it was because there had been no money to buy food, let alone clobber for yet another mouth to feed.

At four o'clock, she took me over herself to see the new baby and all I could see was a red screwed up little face that looked very old and wrinkled. Two little fists were closed tight with thumbs inwards, and every few minutes he would give out a yell as though he was terrified of being catapulted into a strange and alien world. He clung to my Mother like a young terrified monkey. I bent down to kiss him, but he let out a stifled squeak and it was then that noticed that he had no nails on his fingers and I guess none on his toes either, and I suddenly lost all interest in him and longed to go back to Elsie's house and the comfort of the chair by the fire and the egg and bacon butty that had seemed such absolute luxury to me.

10 · *Elsie*

Elsie was our fairy godmother and was always popping over eggs or pies that she had made, sometimes it was a pot of cream that she insisted must be eaten that very day. Bert Storey worked at Poutney's — the pottery that was then in Lodge Causeway. He was an accountant and earned three pounds ten shillings a week compared to Dad's twenty one shillings. He was rich and we were poor. South Road was a typical middle-class road and we had two Councillors and two Doctors living there to prove it. At the bottom of the road was a big house with four big turrets called 'The Towers' and it was always very quiet and select. Most of the children were not allowed in the street to play and sometimes when I threw a rope over a lamp-post for a swing I was told to take it down and move away.

I would slip over to Elsie's quite frequently. Nobody ever asked me where I was going. My Mother had her hands full with the new baby who yelled a lot and wanted all her attention and Denny was locked away in that front parlour — since that dreadful scene I was not allowed to go near them. Elsie always seemed glad to see me and one day she asked me if I would like a book to read. Her only son, David, was a tall, thin lad very much like his mum to look at, but whereas Elsie was vivacious and bright-eyed, he was very shy and would stammer and shuffle. He brought me a book that he had had given to him as a Christmas present and held it out to me at arms length. It was 'Treasure Island' and as I took it from him I asked him if he had read it, but to my surprise he looked even more embarrassed and quietly admitted that he couldn't read. I asked him if he would like me to read it to him and he sat the other side of the fire where I proceeded to bring to life the story of the Hispaniola, Jack Hawkins and that unforgettable character, Long John Silver. Both Elsie and Bert were surprised that I could read so well. They had hired a tutor to teach David but he hadn't achieved a great deal of success. After that, I was a frequent visitor to the house reading to David. Sometimes I would look up from reading to him about some daring cowboy adventure, and he would be behind a chair quietly acting out the story as he listened, and taking careful aim at some unfortunate Indian chief. When he saw that he was being watched by a girl he would become confused and shy. I think in the end, he learned to read in sheer desperation as the tutor kept telling him that his mother or another girl could go on reading to him for ever.

David had a cousin who was a poor relation and who came to stay with him for holidays and sometimes weekends. His name was Bertie and he also had brilliant blue eyes and the most shy and disarming smile. He had fair wavy hair and the most beautiful hands I have ever seen — big and capable and beautiful with square nails that had half-moons showing half an inch long. He was acutely conscious of his shirts which were always torn or had buttons missing. Elsie would dive upstairs and always produce something suitable of David's for him to change

47

into. The three of us would be found in the parlour that in Elsie's house was turned into a study and filled with book cases and a rolled-top desk in the bay window, and it had a green Wilton carpet and brown leather chairs. It was Bert's study, but he never minded us being there and he had a quick, dry sense of humour that made everybody laugh except his wife. It often sent her into hysterics but more from anger than mirth. All this was to come to me in a startling burst of revelation and I was to learn so much more as the pages of my life began to slowly turn, but at that stage I never thought that one day I would wish that I had never set eyes on this fair-haired boy who looked at me so eagerly that I wanted to mother him and when he took my hand to come and read to him, I followed him thinking that for the first time in my life somebody needed me and being able to read was the only thing could do well. Now two people at least respected and admired me and I felt it was the only worthwhile thing I had done in my entire life.

One day at Elsie's house, I picked up a book by Marie Corelli called 'The Mighty Atom', then found another in the library called 'The Sorrows of Satan'. There was a whole series which kept me spellbound. In them she would mention The Ancient Wisdom and I knew I must start on a quest just like the Holy Grail to try to find it. I was like the Watcher on the Tower or the Seeker after Knowledge. Nothing mattered now except to find this wisdom, then I would have the answer to all my problems for hadn't she said, and kept on repeating, that Jesus had said,

'All these things you shall do, and more, if you will only believe.' The book and all that was in it could not lie. It was in the book and so it must be right.

When I told Elsie that I had read all of Marie Corelli's books, she didn't believe me. She said that it was more than she had done and what were they all about? When I discussed them at length, she was amazed and told my Mother that I was a good reader and a very bright little girl . . .

'She's always got her nose in some book or other,' my Mother interrupted, 'I wish sometimes she'd do more for me about the house.'

After that, I had books snatched away from me and I was told to clean the brass or to wash the dishes. Mostly, I had to take the baby out. Clifford as a baby was a very nervous child and cried incessantly, pulling at Mum's skirts until she almost went frantic with agitation. She yelled at him and yelled at me to get him out of her way for ten minutes before she bashed him to death or did him some harm. If Dad tried to comfort her, then her eyes flashed fire and both of us would beat a hasty retreat, Dad to chop firewood and me with Cliff in the pram going purple with rage and frustration until the motion of the pram lulled him off to sleep. That is, until the pram stopped, then he would start again so I had to be perpetually on the move. Sometimes I would take him as far as Tumble Fields which was a favourite spot of ours. We called it that because right in the middle was a big hill that we rolled down or pretended was an unscalable fortress, and half of us defended the fort, and the other half had to attack it. On the other side was the meadow with tall grasses and buttercups and moondaisies. I thought he would love it there just as I had loved once to be in the countryside, oh so long ago now, but when I unstrapped him and hauled him down into the long grass, he screamed and his face went puce with rage and he kept shaking his head from side to side. I wanted to hold him and convey to him that I loved him. I kept remembering all those lonely desperate hours when I too was as desolate as he apparently was. And as his sobs became unbearable to stand any more, I took him in my arms and kissed him telling him that I knew what a strange and alien world he had come into but that I would look after him and that it would be all right. Out of sheer exhaustion, he stopped crying, and suddenly his two little arms reached round my neck and I felt tears wet on his face. I brushed the fair wavy hair now damp

49

from his face and kissed the blue eyes still filled with unshed tears. I yanked the pram out of the tall grass and sat with him on the edge of the field. He stuck a finger in his mouth and still leaning against me closed his eyes and went to sleep. I went to sleep as well and it seemed on that quiet warm afternoon, with the sound of the rooks and the woodpigeons from the copse away over the meadow, dreamed again of that other white bungalow when I had gone to sleep on the verandah to the sounds of the wildlife and the gentle swaying of the trees.

11 · *My Best Friend*

Vera Drinkwater was my best friend. Every morning I would wait for her to come out of Victoria Street. She would be with three other girls, and then together we would all walk to Two Mile Hill School. We shared a burning ambition, finally to court and marry a boy who was clever enough to have passed his exams and gone to Grammar School. Apart from the social upgrading it would bring, was a deep and ingrained desire to be spared the indignities and hardships of our mothers. To be married to a white-collar worker meant less dirty washing, carbisil and washboards. Simple when you stopped to work it out. People higher up the social scale had smaller families and marriage could sound attractive with a man who thought along these lines. All that was a dream of the future though, meanwhile Vee and me were twin souls. We liked the same subjects and worked hard every term to be near the top of the class so we could sit near each other — usually ending up in the top section together as tenth and eighth. We never moved from that top position and we were inseparable. That is, until Bonny Newcliff came.

Bonny hailed from Australia and was a big hefty girl

with a hooked nose and small inquisitive eyes. I was sure she was short-sighted but didn't say so. We were all supposed to make our visitor welcome, and when she was asked one day to write an essay on her life in Australia, I was told to forfeit my break so that I could punctuate and correct the essay. This was a task I found to be well-nigh impossible since she was an atrocious writer and I could hardly decipher the words. The spelling had to be seen to be believed. Bonny had to read the essay aloud. She stood in front of the class with a very stiff neck looking as if she was viewing something from a very long way off and stuttering and going redder by the minute, and finally grinding to an incoherent stop.

Miss Mullan (we all called her Fanny Mullan, but not, of course, to her face) leaned over her desk and sought me out.

'Joyce Dark,' she said, 'I thought you were supposed to correct Bonny's work?'

I remained silent. How could I say in front of everybody that Bonny's essay was a load of ungrammatical and badly spelled rubbish? I looked at Bonny and she was smiling sheepishly. I didn't like her. liked her even less when at break the very next day, there she was talking to Vera, my best friend. For the first time, I experienced jealousy and possessive anger. She was boasting to Vee and a gang of girls round her. She thought we were a load of Pommie cissies; none of us had ever ridden a horse; and there wasn't enough space over here to swing a cat round.

'Why do you stay then?' I was taunted into shouting.

She eyed me with those squinty, piggy eyes.

'Temper, temper.' She laughed, as though she could read my thoughts and knew I would just love to kill her.

Then suddenly I lunged at her and she was still laughing and holding me off with one hand, and I had to stop because I was out of breath.

'Now then, Joycee,' Vee said, 'Watch your manners and be nice to our overseas friend.'

51

'You might be able to ride a horse, but you can't write or spell.' I said to Bonny viciously.

'But can you pick plums?' she asked suddenly.

I was so surprised by this remark that I couldn't reply and stood staring at her stupidly. It was Vee who supplied the answer.

'Bonny and her family have taken over Fry's farm and the orchard, and they want all the help they can get to pick the apples and the plums. We've got half a dozen lads from the Barton, some ladders and you can come on the cart as well if you want to, but make sure you behave yourself.' She said this last with mock severity. I was dumbfounded that all I could say was,

'How kind. How terribly kind.'

Sunday dawned bright and clear. I was sure my prayers had been answered personally because I had fervently clasped my two hands together to ask humbly for a fine day to spend amongst the plums. I rushed over to Vee's house where all was hustle and bustle with the lads loading baskets and ladders onto a horse and cart. The lads hauled me up and tried to do the same with Vee, but she was such a tubby thing in those days they found her to be a bit difficult.

'Struth!' was all they could find time to say.

When we arrived at Fry's farm, we found plenty of activity already going on and the pickers had started on the front trees. Baskets of lush dark red Victorian plums were in rows all along the front porch, and Ma Newcliff in a long skirt and wide-brimmed hat was shouting instructions to a couple of lads about to set a ladder against a tree,

'Get yer asses out of that tree and start on the ones further down,' she yelled.

She was like Bonny, with the same mannish walk and the slight twist of her nose that gave her a prize fighter look. She eyed us both as we came up to her.

'Well,' she said at last, 'I can heave you up (this looking at me) but I ain't so sure about fatso.'

She climbed up the ladder the lad had left beside the tree and then held out her arm and with one mighty swing she hauled me over the lowest branch of an apple tree as easy as pie, then descended again to where Vee stood solid and invincible. I lost sight of them after that. I was in a beloved tree again with lush ripe apples all around me as I picked. I sang softly and was happy up there amongst the leaves and apples with the sun shining through the branches and the sounds of the laughter and muffled conversation of the other pickers.

After that, Bonny was an accepted part of the clan and although I never really liked her, she presented no threat to me after that first rush of unreasonable jealousy. Vee hailed her only as a casual friend along with many others whilst she and I stayed close and shared many secrets.

I was always a little scared of Vee's mother who was a bit of a dragon and famous for her table tapping exploits. Gran Dark said that Ma Drinkwater would call up something she didn't bargain for one day. It was taking things too far, and no good could come of it.

When I called for Vee, I always went round the back way because she was usually in her Father's den. Mr. Drinkwater was a shoemaker by trade and mended shoes for a few extra shillings; he was a poppet and loved us being with him in his den. Vee had a cane basket chair in there which was always piled high with cushions and comics and it was cosy and warm in there from a small stove which Mr. Drinkwater lit when it was cold. He would yarn to us for hours and tell us stories about Kingswood in his day when he was a boy. And there were the tales his father had told him about the olden days when Kingswood had been notorious for footpads, horse thieves and wife bashers His tales about Bristol and Berkeley Castle and. The Chase thrilled and fascinated me as I listened, I could hear again the wheels of the carriages rumble over the rough uneven roads. I could see so clearly the velvet coats and the lace at the wrists of noblemen and the cry of 'Stand and Deliver!' from the masked highwayman. Superstition and the Old Religion and even stone age man was only half buried in those far off days, but I was part of it, and could feel it and it was my past and I belonged to a history that was real. Now it is fast disappearing, swallowed up in a wave of change that will make it vanish completely in a new technological society that sweeps relentlessly onward covering everything and leaving not a trace behind. I am not equipped for this change and one sobering thought as I race against time to relate my story for my children, is that in less than ten years' time, there will be no-one left to tell anybody about those times and the way ordinary people lived.

But back to Harry's den, and Vee's Mother's table-tapping session, sixty years or more ago, and all the family gathered there that night to try to find the riddle of some missing money after the death of Vee's grandmother.

It had grown quite late and Harry Drinkwater had intended to see me home and I was waiting for him to return from delivering a pair of shoes to a neighbour. We were in the corner of the kitchen reading and the entire family on Vee's Mother's side was seated round the table with hands stretched out in front of them and fingers just slightly touching the one sat next to them. One of the relatives sat on one side with a pencil and pad. He was supposed to take the message as it was spelt out. I was reading a serial in the *Schoolgirl* comic and wasn't paying a great deal of notice.

'Is anybody there?' droned Mary, 'Is anybody there?'

The table tilted slightly then came down with a slight thud. It came to me suddenly that if this was a game, it was a very silly game. But if, as Gran Dark had predicted, this was not a game and that Mrs. Drinkwater would call up something one day that she didn't bargain for, then I had no wish to be around and I was suddenly filled with fear and wished Harry would return to take me home. I could now no longer continue to read and sat watching the proceedings with ever-increasing apprehension. The message had to be interpreted by a number of taps, each tap representing a letter of the alphabet. So far, the table had obliged by giving one tap, then four — making A and then D. I half wondered if the players themselves had manoeuvred the jolt, when suddenly the table lifted up almost vertically and then came to rest with a sickening thud. Almost at once, Mary rose to her feet and let out a shriek,

'l knew it,' she yelled, 'I knew it all the time. It was you ADA, — you took the money from your own mother!'

Ada, looking white and shaken, protested her innocence and her husband verified and backed up her statement. Mary, with eyes blazing, lambasted her sister and called her all the names under the sun. It was at this point that Harry arrived and stopped the proceedings with a few well-chosen words. He told the company to go and he said,

'I'll not have these ungodly goin's on in my house.' And looking over at me, he said,

'Now, my Queen, let's get you home.'

The street lights were cool white pools of comfort, as we walked the short distance to my house, but I was surprised to learn it was almost midnight and hoped I would be able to slip inside without waking my parents. The key to the front door always hung on a long piece of string behind it, so that all I had to do was to pull it through the letterbox. The stairs creaked a bit as I ascended them and I had carefully to avoid the well-known offending ones. I reached the safety of my bedroom and switched on the light. The naked bulb at the end of the long piece of flex was swinging slightly to and fro in the draught from the window which was open at the top. I shivered as I began to undress and remembered the events of the night. I began to feel some unknown evil had followed me home. Vee's Mum had been wrong to take things so far. There were things you could do and things you could not. Everybody knew that.

55

Just supposing she had called up something evil, and it had followed me home. I remembered my Sunday School teacher telling us one day that the Devil never bothered with evil people because they were his already. Then it struck me that I wasn't good either. Aunt Ada said that I was a bad bitch, and I had already been sent away, so it would be easy for Old Nick to keep company with me. I would be the Devil's Disciple and he would be coming to enlist my help to destroy other souls. My heart was thumping now. I could hear it as twisted about in my iron bed. How I wished that I had found The Ancient Wisdom that Marie Corelli had spoken about in her books! Then I would know everything, even how to banish evil and reach upward to the light.

The clock tower began to chime midnight — the Witching Hour — this was the time things went bump in the night. I held my breath and waited for the last chime to die away and just at that split second, the light bulb gave a slight click and went out and a great black mass jumped on to my bed . . . I was suddenly screaming my head off and shouting incoherently.

'I'll be good, I'll be good, I'll be good. Oh please don't let the Devil have me, I'll be good.'

My Father appeared from nowhere, still wearing his white longjohns and button-at-the-neck vest.

'Had a bad dream, my babby?' he said, brushing the cat from my bed, 'Shall Dad make ya a nice cuppa tea?' 'Yes,' I said, letting him think it had been a nightmare, yet still wanting to prolong the presence of another human being, 'The — the light's gone out,' I spluttered, 'The light's gone.'

'Dad'll put in a new one tomorrow.'

'No, now.' I stated firmly.

'If Dad can find one downstairs.' His voice trailed off as he manoeuvred the dark stairs. I heard the steps creak as he made his way down. I heard the kitchen door open and then silence as the darkness descended on the room again. I closed my eyes tight, for it seemed that cold phantom hands still reached out to grab me.

12 · *A Bun Dance*

An incident happened a few weeks later, to convince me that the path of goodness was not an easy one to follow. If I must strive upwards on the way to salvation, I would need all my brains and wits to get there. I made one other startling discovery: grown-ups did not always say what they meant. I had encountered the same dilemma with the roughnecks on the Patch. Their most powerful answer to a question they wanted to evade was,

'Whaat?'

Grown-ups would usually say,

'What are you talking about? Go and play.'

I was thinking about all this on that morning I met up with Vee walking to school. That term had been wonderful and we had for the first and only time received equal marks, which meant we were sitting in the same desk together. My joy was complete. We filed into our classroom to the lively strains of the March Militaire We were sixth and seventh top girls in the class and sat half-way up the aisle in the top section. I had now acquired a little knack of tossing back my curls just to acknowledge this slight air of superiority. My pride was to receive a fall that day. As well as being full of sin, I was puffed up with pride as well. The moment had not as yet come, so the curls bobbed again as I lifted the lid of my desk to take out the English Writing Book in which we were to have our first lesson of the day in Copperplate Handwriting.

Miss Morgan, our teacher, wore tortoiseshell framed glasses and constantly picked her nose. She had a habit of picking up a ruler and thwacking it on the back of your hand the exact number of times she wanted to emphasize something, like history dates, for example. At the same time, she would push her nose and glasses right into your face so that you could see her nostrils dilate like a bull about to charge. It would go something like this:

'1066 to 1087' Thwack, thwack.
'1087 to 1100' Thwack, thwack.
'1100 to 1132' Thwack, thwack.

A vein on the back of my hand would suddenly appear like a small knot in a rope and cause excruciating pain. She would then command in sharp, stacatto tones,

'What were they?'

Half paralysed with pain and fear, my mind would go blank, and nothing but a wave of relief at the dull subsiding of pain ever emerged from those encounters, and yet, after all these years that repetition technique has never failed suddenly to produce some useless piece of data from those far off school days.

Miss Morgan closed the register and lightly clasped her hands in front of her. She surveyed us for a minute or two, then taking a piece of chalk she wrote the word ABUNDANCE in large capitals on the blackboard. Underneath, she drew two thick lines, then proceeded to transform the same word into copperplate handwriting, giving the A in Abundance the most extravagant and dramatic tail. My head swirled and the letter seemed to come alive like a courtier in green velvet breeches and big plumed hat, that he now took off with a great wide sweep so that the plumed feather swept the floor with the expansive sweep of the tail of the A.

We had to copy what she had written and later it would be marked according to merit. I loved this flowery writing. To me it was exciting and romantic, a far cry from the untidy and almost indecipherable scrawl you see today. Another lost art, like brass moulding, my father would have said.

I had long since finished and was sitting idly watching the others scribbling laboriously away. Some of them leaning over their books with pink tongues peeping from the corners of their mouths. The word ABUNDANCE conjured up for me A BUN DANCE and I began to draw three happy little buns complete with currants and blue bows dancing a jig. Tra la la, Tra la la, came a little caption out of their mouths and I beat a soft tattoo on the desk top to keep time with it, Tra la la.

Vee glanced up from her work and saw what I had done. Recognition dawned, and she stifled a snigger and the girl behind her popped her head up to see what was going on. Vee passed the bit of paper behind her, and a whole series of sniggers and loud giggles followed. It had progressed half way round the classroom before Miss Morgan became aware that the calm of the lesson was being ruffled. Then with a voice like thunder at the crack of doom, she bellowed,

'WELL?'

A tall, lanky girl with buck teeth like a rabbit uncurled her length from the desk, looking awkward and sheepish standing there, holding the offending piece of paper in her hand. She delivered my death knell in one direct blow.

'Please Miss, Joyce Dark did this.'

She extended my stroke of genius at arms length, whilst Miss Morgan advanced to the centre aisle. They met and the three little buns changed hands. After a cursory glance at it and with a contemptuous slight curl of her upper lip, it was torn into shreds and committed to the waste paper basket. Miss Morgan's big owl eyes turned on me.

'Come out here,' she commanded and I wished I was a snail so that I could have retreated beneath the bony structure of a shell, and defied all attempts at being coaxed or cajoled into coming out. Escape was impossible. I knew her next command before it came. 'Fetch the cane.'

The cane was always kept by Miss Dugdale's desk which was on a raised dais in the middle of the hall. The burning humiliation was, that you not only had to fetch your torture, you had to carry it back to the classroom and return it to its place after your punishment. And to bear the sting of wounded pride by being caned in front of forty pairs of curious and sadistic eyes. When a girl fetched the cane, Miss Dugdale never asked why. She took it for granted that such matters were justified if the teacher deemed it so. Miss Dugdale had bunions, so she walked stiffly and painfully behind me with an expression that seemed to say,

'This will hurt me as much as it hurts you.'

Not a foot scraped the floor, or desk banged, or a cough broke the silence as the cane was raised high in the air and then brought down hard. Once, twice, and then for a third time on to my outstretched palm. I gave only a slight gasp as she indicated that I raise the other hand for a further three strokes. I nursed my smarting palms beneath my armpits as she drew herself to her full height and disclosed to the whole class that I was a disruptive influence, a state of affairs that could not and would not be allowed to go on.

I could feel the weal from the smack of the cane begin to rise on my hands, and didn't know how I would carry the cane back to its resting place beside the Head-mistress's desk, where I would have to stand for the rest of the morning as a spectacle for the whole school to gaze upon. With a concentrated effort to control my tears, I took the offending cane she was now wiggling in front of me, and proceeded to follow her. The head girl, Gwen Monks, who was also door monitoress, rushed from her seat to open the door for her, and she sailed imperiously through and I trailed miserably behind.

As I stood there in that vast hall, I was filled with dark and dire thoughts. Teachers, grown-ups and parents were all too difficult to understand, and if I was as bad as they all made out — well, I wasn't even going to try to be good any more. I would be as bad as they made me out to be. Even God was hard to find, even though in 'The Ancient Wisdom' Marie Corelli had assured every-body that all you had to do was talk to God, just like you spoke to your own father. It did occur to me at that moment that I wasn't at all sure that my Father might not respond to the Ancient Wisdom in the same way that he responded to Elsie Storey being Liberal, but I thought I ought to give God a chance to intervene on my behalf which He did with the most surprising result.

13 · *Red Letter Day*

Ever since the discovery of the Marie Corelli books, I had taken a renewed interest in Sunday School, the Band of Hope and other chapel activities. Sometimes I went three times on a Sunday. thought that if anybody knew anything about this subject, it would be there that I would learn about it. I usually went to sleep during the Sermon, which went on for an interminably long time, and only woke up with a start when the Right Reverend somebody or other banged his fist on the pulpit to call on all us miserable sinners to repent. In fact, quite a lot of people woke up with a start, and I reckon he did it on purpose. Anyway, I was very pleased that God thought us all miserable sinners because that meant grown-ups were no better than me. I had also taken to reading the New Testament. I tried starting off with the Old, but got lost in a maze of Begetting but didn't like that very much because it sounded not at all nice. I had another reason for perusing the Good Book.

At school, we had a lesson called Religious Instruction which I liked. The few weeks prior to my fateful humiliation, the Vicar of All Saints Church just below the school had visited us one morning when we were all assembled in the hall, and had presented us with the news that there was to be a bible presented to the girl who could correctly answer questions about the bible, and write an essay on a story from the bible. I had entered for that, and on that morning as stood in the hall with my heart full of dark thoughts, I had already made up my mind that I would ask my Mother to intercede with the teachers on my behalf. Maybe if she could explain to them that hadn't meant any harm, that I had finished first and was only filling in time it would be alright. After all, it wasn't my fault that Vee had giggled, and then passed those three little buns around the class.

I told my Mother, at dinner time, I showed her my hands where the weals were now turning purple.

'You shouldn't mess about at school. You go there to learn.'

'But will you see my teacher?' I pleaded.

'I don't know, I'll have to think about it,' was all she had to say and I had to leave it at that.

During that afternoon my punishment for being a disruptive influence was completed. I was removed from my coveted eighth place in the top section and made to sit with the backward section at the very bottom of the class. Oh, the bitter, bitter shame of it! How would I ever be able to hold my head high again? I would rather have had six more slashes with the cane than this crushing and unutterable blow descend upon me.

All the dunces in this bottom section conveyed their commiserations to me, and to their everlasting credit, one or two even whispered,

'Aaah.'

A couple of them smiled at me and Ivy Dickson who was known as being 'as thick as two short planks' and who was now my desk mate whispered confidentially,

'Ye kin sit by the radiator if ye like.'

With my chin lowered on to my chest, I even ignored a hand that came from Vera Beek and squeezed my arm reassuringly. In my imagination I wanted some unseen power to rescue me from all this humiliation that seemed like a bad dream. I even sat and fantasised that Rudolf Valentino complete with black cape flying in the wind and white bournoose about his head was already galloping across the playground on his white arab steed, and would presently climb up on to the window sill and carry me away. To music, of course.

62

I knew my Mother had come because Miss Morgan was summonsed suddenly away by Miss Dugdale herself, accompanied by the frantic leapings of Gwen the head girl rushing to open the door. My heart did a mad tattoo and I kept thinking,

'Now it will be all over and everything will be as it was.'

Miss Morgan returned and there was a sardonic smile on her face. She looked triumphantly over at me and said in cold, calculating tones,

'Even your own Mother had to admit she had more trouble with you than her two boys put together.'

God, and Rudolf Valentino, seemed very far away from me at that moment.

When I rushed into the kitchen that night, I could hardly speak to my Mother. She had betrayed me and I was filled with anger. She looked at my sullen face and demanded to know what other mischief I had got myself into.

'You didn't have to tell Miss Morgan that I was more trouble than both Den or Cliff put together,' I said. Then recklessly I stormed on, 'You never see Dennis, and Cliff you want out of your sight as much as possible.'

I stopped when I saw the blank expression on her face. 'I meant,' she said, 'Illness wise — I had a lot of trouble with you when you were little.'

She didn't continue but said in a kinder tone,

'Come and have your tea, nothing lasts for ever, and it will be alright tomorrow you'll see.'

The next day I made my way to the bottom section still with a sinking heart. The only people glad to see me were the dunces who greeted me like a long-lost friend and Vera even gave me her lunch which consisted of two pieces of cold toast wrapped in greaseproof paper with her name written on the front. I was instructed to teach them how to read, a task well-nigh impossible. They laboured over every word and in desperation, I produced a comic, sat them all in a circle and read to them the adventures of Tiger Tim. I was defiant now and so reckless I didn't care if I was caught or not. There was nothing more they could do to me, and the rapt look on all those faces gave me a warm and thrilling feeling. The smell of chalk and dust, cold toast and jam sandwiches filled the classroom and I was still Queen of the Dunces and what was more, their beloved one at that.

The fact that I was wasting time away from my own subjects bothered me a bit, but not much. There was a kind of freedom down here at the bottom of the heap, no pushing or striving to compete. found it relaxing and agreeable. Nobody bothered you and exam marks were not expected of you either. It wasn't that I didn't care. I cared desperately, but I was gradually becoming resigned to the fact that if no-one else cared, why should I? Events were moving to a sudden climax though, and all to my benefit . . .

We were all assembled in the hall, for this was the day the Vicar of All Saints Church was coming to announce the winner of the best bible story and a correct question and answer entry from the New Testament. All the teachers twittered and made a great fuss when the Vicar came into the hall and made his way to the platform. He wore his long black vestment over which his white surplice and black cross looked so impressive and holy. I felt I had no business to be there at all. I tried to look as insignificant as possible. He began by saying that he wished to thank all those who had responded so magnificently to this competition and how delighted he was that so many young minds were seeking the Lord's Words.

With our coming entry into the world of work and adulthood, he was sure that this basic religious training would stand us all in good stead.

'I know,' he went on, 'That you are all waiting for me to announce the winner of the coveted Bible, but before I do, I want to say one thing about the composition that was so outstanding that it warranted the prize on its merit alone. It was the story of Martha and Mary, told in such a way that it brought tears to my eyes.'

He got quite carried away, and his voice rose to a pitch as though he were delivering a sermon.

'She,' he continued, 'Who had chosen the better part (and his voice fell again) and sat and listened to the words of Our Saviour, the Lord Jesus Christ. I proudly present this Bible to Joyce Dark. A most outstanding achievement and a most remarkable girl.'

There was a moment of almost stunned silence, then applause that carried me forward to receive my prize. God had answered my prayers. I had believed that it would all come right and it had. As I passed Miss Morgan she looked slightly sick. At least, that is what I hoped she would feel and I allowed myself that superior toss of my curls just as I passed her and my head was now held high. For who could ever again call me bad or disruptive when religion and the Lord and the Vicar were on my side?

The very next day, I regained my seat in the top section and all my friends in the bottom section by the radiator waved and smiled to me. I had learned my first lesson in wisdom, old or new. To be a fine, upstanding, respected member of the community — write a composition or get to know the Vicar. I still remember the rendering of 'The Lord is my Shepherd' that I gave to the school with all my most dramatic appeal, and the heady feeling of elation when I saw such approval on the Vicar's face. When he finally dismissed me with a blessing, these words flashed though my mind,

'And greater things shall ye do, if ye will only believe.'

I insisted on being Christened after that, for it was a sad fact that this simple ceremony had been neglected. if you were not Christened, you would not enter into The Kingdom of Heaven when you died. To be the grand age of ten years old before this special event took place was an occasion not to be missed, especially as Ada and Flo decided that Denny shouldn't miss out on anything that was going free. So the whole family turned up at Sunday School that afternoon in our best clobber, with me in a white dress with three frills round the bottom looking like an oversized Shirley Temple, with a whacking great white bow on the back of my six brown curls. The kids bawled out their signature tune that announced the opening session:

'We're little tiny pilgrims
Our hearts are gay,
We're very fond of singing
To cheer the way.
Chorus:
To cheer the way, to cheer the way,
There's nothing like a happy song, to cheer the way.'

This was sung with great gusto, and when they had finished they sat down with a great scraping of feet, some even deciding to lift their chairs and transport them to another location, until Mr. Shepherd, the Superintendent, walked in and held up his hands for silence. Aunt Flo and Aunt Ada were making sure Den's hair was tidy and his tie was straight. Den was trying to wriggle away from them and managed to disentangle himself and stand by Dad, just as a large handkerchief was produced by Ada and moved towards his face to wipe his nose. He gave a loud and audible sniff. My Mother frowned and Dad leaned over to take the handkerchief and passed it to his son who promptly blew his nose with great gusto and handed it back to Aunt Ada. When this operation had been completed, Mr. Shepherd cleared his throat and said,

'Let us pray.'

We all bowed our heads and said The Lord's Prayer, after which he told everybody to be very silent because this was a solemn and sober time when two of God's children were going to pledge themselves into His keeping for ever and ever. Someone brought some water in an earthenware bowl. He dipped his fingers into the bowl and splashed some water on my head making the sign of the Cross,

'In the Name of the Father, . . .' he droned and then went on to do the same to Dennis. A drop of water fell onto my nose and into my mouth and it tasted like rain water and not a bit holy. After that, the class sang once more, 'What a friend we have in Jesus' and I was now well on the way to Salvation. From now on, Jesus loved me and I was protected night and day by this band of love. Like a soldier, was armed to face the great big world and as I stepped forward to face the unknown, like the Fool in the Tarot pack I did not see the pitfalls, nor did I care.

14 · *The Flicks*

After that, I confided to Vee that I might eventually become a Nun. She scoffed at the idea and said,

'Oh come on, Joyce! You wouldn't like it kneeling on a stone floor every day praying for hours. Besides, think of the holes you would wear in your stockings.'

I immediately thought of the darns I had in the only two pairs of black stockings I possessed and nodded soberly at this practical approach. Then she nudged me confidentially and whispered, 'We're going to the flicks tonight. Coming?'

I nodded. *Ben Hur* was at the local bug house and to get a seat for this great epic, I would have to bolt down my tea and queue with Vee and her family. If you were lucky, you could get into the first few rows of the sevenpences which came halfway up the hall and just right to be able to see the silver screen without cricking your neck. Right next to the cinema was a sweet shop with bottles of sweets and an array of mouth-watering chocolates for sixpence a quarter. Courting couples usually got the chocs, and they always sat in the balcony seats at one and thruppence. Of course, this luxury depended on whether you were lucky enough to be going out with a young man who was in work, otherwise the pictures were out and a walk round the park would have to suffice. Everybody who could afford it, went to the pictures every week. Even the kids went on Saturday afternoon. This cost us three whole pence and was our pocket money for the week. *Ben Hur* had been blazoned on bill posters for weeks. With a cast of thousands, it was supposed to be sensational, and special sound effects had been acquired at great expense.

The talkies were about to burst upon us, but the silent films were still with us and those who couldn't read the captions often had plenty of people around them to supply the story they missed. There would be long sighs and cries of 'Aaah' when the villain of the piece did his dirty deeds, and as the film was projected onto the screen, the beam from the cinematograph poured down through a thick haze of pipe and tobacco smoke that we coughed and spluttered through in order to see our favourite actors appear on the screen. Janet Gaynor, Charles Farrel, Frederic March, Douglas Fairbanks, Norma Shearer, Noel Beery were just a few of these. They took us into another world of glamour and romance, and escape from the harsh drab reality of our lives. As schoolgirls, we copied hairstyles and tried to emulate them. The false became the real.

But no film could start before the pianist arrived. He was the most important man in those far off days of silent movies. When he arrived at the cinema, and began to walk down the faded red-carpeted aisle, claps, whistles and foot scuffling would accompany him all the way down to the cinema pit where his grand piano always stood. It was his inspired playing that could bring a lump to your throat when our hero was nigh unto death and our heroine ministered to him, or filled you with fear and trepidation when Indians charged the stage coach, or prompted you to rise in your seats to urge the hero to sock the villain to death, or kick his teeth in, and to boo and shout until we were hoarse.

The night of *Ben Hur* was a night to remember, for as well as the pianist, we had a three-piece band. The noise was deafening as cymbals crashed their way through the great chariot race; drums rolled when the Christians were fed to the lions and I couldn't help thinking of the Vicar of All Saints Church being among the first batch if he had lived in those dreadful times. The band, the film and the moment etched itself indelibly on my mind. It's as though I have only to open a door and everything is there in a silent dusty cupboard of memories, ready to come alive once more.

The talking pictures arrived. They had built a new cinema at the Kingsway and Vee and I screamed and held on to each other when the pale horse of death seemed to leap out of the screen and on to us. Everything was larger than life and full of energy and movement.

We raced down to the new cinema before school one morning just to gaze at a large poster outside the cinema with Carlotta King dancing in a flame coloured dress and John Bowles in flowing Arab headgear singing in *The Desert Song*, standing there in the rain in rapt attention, then turning and running all the way back to the school gates with the bell ringing madly in our ears. Out' of breath, and just making it to school in time, we whispered to each other as we filed into our classroom that we would go on Friday night to see it, because Saturday would be so crowded and we might have to queue for hours. Friday, we could go straight from school so long as we let our parents know. We could take sandwiches, call on a couple of mates who lived down that way and then we would be ready to be first in the queue for the evening performance.

Oh, the never-to-be-forgotten thrill of that colourful musical, and how our hearts almost stopped beating at the romance and the marvellous songs! We lived in a dream world for weeks afterwards.

The books from the school library were discarded. *Ann of Green Gables*, *Good Wives* and *Little Women* were abandoned, and in their place every week, hot off the press we raced to the newsagent's to get our copy of *Peg's*

Paper. This we kept under our desks and sneaked out at opportune moments to read about tragic heroines whose husbands left them on their wedding nights, or about attractive servant girls who were so virtuous and sweet that they married a Lord, or the Boss of a big concern. In the back of my mind, I was convinced that the Ancient Wisdom was at work again, and just as the men earnestly believed that there would be a brighter tomorrow, so we as young girls believed that something like a miracle would happen to lift us out of our poverty. So films like *Pygmalion* which portrayed a kind of 'rags to riches' theme became firm favourites with us.

15 · *Douglas's Sports Day*

Once a year, and sometimes on my birthday, which is 23rd July, Douglas's, the famous motorbike factory at the bottom of our street, held their annual sports day. From two o'clock onwards, South Road was crowded with people all converging on to the sports field, queuing up at four payboxes then squeezing through the turnstiles and on to the field. There were cycle races, and new motor bike displays, athletics and all kinds of events — enough to bring the World and His Wife out to watch, to cheer and to clap and enjoy a day of days. I had never been. Like a lot of the other children, we hung around the payboxes in the forlorn hope that a friend or a relative might turn up and take us in with them. Nobody ever did, but optimism was always on our side in those days.

When the events were over, and the days takings tallied and removed with a Bobby as escort, the gates were left open for anybody to come in for the Fair and the final display of fireworks. The fireworks didn't come on until eleven o'clock, and we had to get permission to stay out so long. However, we were through the gates as soon as we saw the last man in the ticket box move out, and across the fenced-off area where the races and heats had taken place.

The lads would be on the lookout for empty ciggy packets so that they could extract the shiny new cigarette cards we called 'generals'. We all saved series of them from wild flowers to film stars. When each series was completed, we stretched a rubber band around the pile and they were packed jealously away. Lads exchanged 'twicers' for cards they did not have; this was a serious before-school activity and could not be hurried or interfered with. Girls too, joined in the search to help with their brothers, although they did not save the cards nor share in the excitement that the boys felt.

Beyond the sports ground, was the field where the Fair was. At six-thirty, the big wurlitzer on the merry-go-round would begin to blare out the lively tunes that could be heard all over the fairground and half way up the street. Everything would come alive, with crowds of people all milling around, shouting and jostling one another in a good-natured way. I was going to ask my Mother to take me on the helter-skelter tonight. I had never been on it yet and I cherished a dream of manoeuvring all those steps right to the top, then to close my eyes and come down on the mat.

'Please take me,' I pleaded, 'Just once, and late enough to see the fireworks as well.'

My Mother did not seem too eager to comply.

'I'll have to get Cliff to bed first, but be by the helter-skelter at nine-thirty,' she grudgingly said.

I couldn't wait to get back to the Fairground and tonight my cherished dream was coming true. I hugged myself and tried to picture what it would be like speeding down the steep slope of the helter-skelter. I wandered from stall to stall watching people try their hand at throwing a small light wooden hoop over various prizes. It was more difficult than it looked, and not a soul

71

managed to do it when I was watching. I wandered on and was drawn to the big wurlitzer. The great horses were moving up and down as if prancing, and leaping to the time of the music. The man on the steps wore a top hat and tailcoat and seemed to be conducting the music; he whistled shrilly and the children waved to him as they bobbed up and down and sped round and round. It was all so merry and gay and I wished I was up there with them.

Presently there was a stir in the crowd as one of the stewards selling tickets walked past me with about a dozen kids following him. The reason became clear, because to my utter amazement, he suddenly tore off a whole strip of tickets and threw them into the crowd of children who blocked his way at every step. The kids swooped on the tickets and fought to gain possession of them whilst the young steward took the opportunity to escape. I stood watching the lads still grovelling in the mud, having a free-for-all for the coveted blue strips. Then I moved closer to the tall tower of the helter-skelter with its twinkling lighted tip and the spiraling turns and twists that I longed to slide down. In the twilight of a warm summer evening, the brightness of the Fair, with the endless rows of different coloured bulbs, gave it the air of Christmas. I wished my Mother would appear, Cliff was often difficult to persuade to go to sleep. Sometimes, Mum had to stay with him for hours and then he would start to cry as soon as she left the room. Perhaps she wouldn't be able to get away at all. I tried not to think of that.

Out of the corner of my eye I saw the young steward come round again, still with a crowd of youngsters following. On impulse, I followed them making sure that I kept to the back of the lads. Boys were noisy and I was timid of any aggression. I wanted to be sure of a quick exit in case any scrabbling took place. I saw the young man suddenly pull back his arm to throw a stream of tickets in the air. They landed square in the middle of the boys who surged forward to retrieve them. It was then that I noticed him feel in his pockets and pull out something else. Something which then whizzed through the air and fell with a soft thud! right against my chest and rolled into my cardigan. I pulled out the thin end of a whole row of tickets. There must have been fourteen at least. It was the end of the roll.

I moved quickly out of sight so that nobody could follow me. I had a quick glimpse of a small boy who had seen the whole thing and was now looking shyly and enquiringly at me. As long as he didn't give me away, I thought, and moved quickly out of earshot. When I looked back, he was obviously so disconsolate and fed up, that he was knocking the heads off flowers with his boots. I had first thought that I would spend the whole fourteen tickets continually going on the helter-skelter. I didn't want to glance back at him so waited for him to come level with me. He didn't want to catch my eye. He was no doubt wishing that he had been the one to have caught those precious slips. We were now by the shiny horses bobbing up and down on the merry-go-round. He stayed by my side until they slowed down.

'Want a ride?' I said.

His eyes lit up, 'Yeeah' was all he replied.

We both ran to grab at the massive monsters and clung on tightly to the brass bar that rose from their backs like great bars of gleaming gold. The music started up again and I watched the heads of the crowds whizz past like faceless phantoms. When I closed my eyes the music shrieked loud and shrill until it seemed that there was only me and the music blaring in that giddy merry-go-round. When it was all over, we slipped from our steeds, raced down the steps and over to the swing boats. We were holding hands now, a roll of tickets had made us friends. I too wanted the companionship of another sharing the excitement of a fair. We tried the chair'o'planes and then the dodgems. Soon I knew I would make my way to the helter-skelter. The last four tickets I would not share. He had known instinctively when he had been shown the remaining blue slips that my intention was not to share any more with him. He hadn't remonstrated with me or even looked disappointed. He had just kicked at the ground, smiled that shy smile turned, and melted away. The last adventure was mine to savour alone.

The stars were out now, and I grabbed a mat and started up the steps to that tall tower. When I reached the top I stopped to look at the whole panorama. I was like a giant looking down on all the world. I set the mat at just the right angle. I had anticipated exactly what it would be like. The mad exhilarating thrill as each corner was rounded on the descent, down-sliding with increasing speed until the final spin off at the end. Then the repeat journey up the steps and the same thrill as I did it four times in a row. I was not disappointed. When the final ticket had been collected, and I had for the last time flipped myself skilfully off the ledge on to the big mat beneath, I gave a big sigh of satisfaction. I had had a wonderful hour, full of surprises. I was still standing there gazing up at the stars, when my Mother pushed her way towards me.

'Come on . . . she said in agitation, 'Just one ride and no more.' I opened my mouth to tell her of the joy of the last hour, but the music and noise was too loud, so I simply followed her up to the top of the tower. I let her go first so that I could savour the thrill all over again by myself. When I reached the bottom my Mother was holding her shoe which she had taken off. Her face was as black as thunder.

'I've lost the bloody heel of my shoe through you wanting to ride on that damned thing, ' she grumbled. 'It's long past your bedtime anyway,' she went on, 'so come home now before something else happens.'

She put on her shoe but walked like a woman with a wooden leg all the way home.

16 · *The Curse*

I was just past my tenth birthday and was idly playing with Cliff in the backyard. I was trying to read a book and play with him at the same time. He was bringing me small stones which he said were 'taties' and he wanted me to wrap them up so that he could take them home for din-din. I was the shop-keeper. He would dig in his pocket for imaginary money, and I would peer over my book to tell him that there were no spuds left, they were all sold out. Then the tiny stones were produced and dumped on my book with an emphatic 'taties' and the game would start all over again.

I felt slightly irritated and did not really want to play. Moreover, my head was muzzy and the tops of my legs ached. In the pit of my stomach there was a dull, persistent pain that I suddenly realised had been there for several days. I had previously placed a cushion and a rug on the patch of earth that served as a yard, but along the back wall there was now a brave row of bronze tiger lilies that Dad had carefully nurtured, standing tall and regal blaring their autocratic appearance to the world like a small line of heraldic trumpets. In Autumn there would be Michaelmas Daisies and Golden Rod and Asters in their miriad colours. There were Geraniums in boxes on the wall, but no grass ever grew in the centre of that patch. I never remembered one blade. The hard ground beneath my thin body became increasingly uncomfortable. Finally, I got up and went indoors, with Cliff howling dismally at the loss of this shopkeeper and playmate.

I had to lie down. The desire to curl up in bed with a hot water bottle, even though it was day was too strong to be ignored. Dad always carried powders around with him in his breast pocket. He could swallow a powder down in one gulp without water. They were like

Beechams Powders. I found one easily in his jacket behind the door and struggled to get it down by drinking a long draught of water, but it stuck in my throat and I began to choke and gasp. I washed my face under the tap which made me feel cold all over so that I longed more than ever for the comfort of the blankets and the hot bottle on my aching limbs. Sometime later I crawled between the warm flanelette sheets and felt the heat of the bottle which, together with the effect of the powder lulled me into a fitful slumber until the pain gradually subsided and my legs ceased to feel heavy.

When I awoke, my Mother was standing over me. She had several strange objects in her hands, in her mouth were two large safety pins and a length of white tape hung round her neck. I thought at first she was about to dust the room when I saw that she was holding what seemed to be a white piece of cloth in her hands. I was surprised when she curtly asked me to get out of bed and then began to inspect the place where I had lain. A dark stain, like brown shoe-polish lay in the curve of the sheeting and I saw my Mother give a tiny nod to indicate that she had found what she was looking for. In that first startled moment, I honestly thought that the tell-tale marks had actually come from me slipping beneath the covers with my shoes still on. Now I was going to be told off for making work for her.

'I didn't wear my shoes in bed, Mum, honest.'

She gave me a mirthless little half-laugh, then hurried on almost breathlessly,

'You will get this feeling every month now, and you will bleed. I want you to wear this (pointing to the cloth and giving me the pins). From now on, you must not play with boys, and you must keep your skirts down in front of your brothers. That's all you need to know.' Then she said in a kinder tone,

'I shall get you a cup of tea, and I should stay in bed if I were you.' I opened my mouth to say something, to ask a thousand questions, but realised that my Mother was embarrassed. She was gone from the room before I could ask her what to do with the piece of tape and the two safety pins.

'I did not take kindly to 'the curse' and it was Elsie who filled me in with details of what every woman should know.

The rows, and there were plenty in our house, were never physical. They were verbal battles in which my Mother in her quiet way would always come off best, with my Father retreating and Ada being dragged by Flo back to the front room. Denny too, would scuttle like a scared rabbit into this harbour and the door would be locked behind him. Peace at all costs, was the motto of the two men of the house. I got used to the interchange of words, and from the vantage point of the arm of the big wooden chair on which I sat perched like an umpire at a tennis match, I could view the opponents and guess with certainty at which stage the battle would be won and which protagonist would retreat.

I must admit to a certain feeling of elation, and afterwards I would rehearse imaginary conversations with clever people where my own arguments were erudite and witty.

Elsie would sometimes drop in, in the middle of one of Dad's table-thumping sessions. She'd come into the kiichen looking slightly scared at my Father's violent attempt at lucidity. He seemed always to be slightly antagonistic towards her, especially when she brought my Mother things. I think it secretly hurt him that he could not provide all the extra little luxuries and he had no wish to be grateful to anybody. Elsie was too good-natured to have any motive other than the desire to be a good friend, so she would slide into the room and wait for Dad to cool down. Her silence infuriated him even further and he would rant on about the bloody Tories and fat-gutted archy-bishops. My Mother would make a sign to Elsie to remain silent and sitting down by my Mother she would exclaim, 'Well! What's brought all this on?'

Joyce's Mum and Dad

'Bloody Tories!' My Father would explode, 'Capitalists exploiting the workers!'

'Depends which way you look at things.' Elsie said coolly. 'There is another point of view. There are, after all, plenty of opportunities for those who are prepared to work hard to get there.'

'Liberal!' shouted my Father as though it were a dirty word, 'You might as well be a bloody Tory. Bloody turncoats, that's what they are! And tell me just where are these equal opportunities? You know as well as I do it's money that decides what education you get, and it's education that decides what job you get.'

Elsie, now red-faced and angry, would explain how David, her son, was still studying hard at school whilst other lads were earning money. How he would forfeit seven long years of his life to obtain his cherished degree. And did my Father not think that all this sacrifice was worth the financial rewards that it would bring? She and Bert neither smoked nor drank, did not go on holiday, and Bert had got his firm to keep back each rise, so that at the end of the year, it went straight to pay off the school fees.

She finally lifted an accusing finger at him and said, 'You talk of opportunities yet it has never crossed your mind what a bright little girl you have, and what you could do for her. You do nothing but holler and shout.'

My Mother bit her lip, and Dad left the room beaten by the power of Elsie's words and defeated by his own inability to express himself. But it was a battle of words that went on for years between them; between two people with opposing points of view and in their own way, I think they actually enjoyed it.

As for me, I wished that Elsie had been my Mother, and all the things in that house were mine, including the long road to learning which would have been a reality and not a dream. I suddenly leaned over and kissed her.

17 · *Uncle John*

From time to time, various members of my Father's family would descend upon us. They would all come with the excuse that they needed to know how Chas was, and then make no attempt to leave. My Mother still maintained that the whole Dark family was as mad as March hares and resigned herself to listening to a load of drivel, as she said, and trying to urge them to return home because she hadn't any room and couldn't house or feed them. It was on a cold February day, when little flurries of snow made powdery white patches everywhere, that Dad's only brother, John, appeared and banged on the back door. He was clad only in a thin suit with no hat and wearing a green muffler around his neck and a pair of mittens with more holes than fingers on his hands. When he was admitted, he made his way straight to the big wooden arm chair in front of the fire and held his hands to the blaze. He enquired how Dad was, and after that fell silent but remained a fixture, never budging from that prime position by the warm range. Later that night, Mum suggested that he ought to make tracks to go home,

'I should go now, John, before the weather gets any worse.' To this, his only reply was,

"Ud 'ee, Nell?'

'Aah,' my Mother replied, lifting her eyes to heaven, 'I 'ud.'

John went on smoking some evil smelling tobacco in a clay pipe. It was obvious he was settled and quite happy. My Mother was not happy. She made a bed up for him on a mattress in the sitting room. Every morning when we came down he would still be there. Finally, he would get up and sit in the chair by the fire drinking endless cups of tea and eating pieces of toast and dripping. Occasionally, Ada would stop to have a few words with her brother. But apart from the monosyllabic 'Aah' and 'Noo', he went on silently puffing on his old clay pipe.

After several weeks of this, my Mother began in desperation to consult the newspaper for vacant jobs and inveigle him into trying for one,

80

'This one sounds quite good,' she would say with enthusiasm, 'I should try for that.'

''Ud 'ee, Nell?'

This was his only reply amidst clouds of smoke that made everybody cough and splutter, but which seemed to have no effect on him whatsoever.

'The Workhouse!' my Mother exploded one morning several weeks later when it was apparent that she had had enough of the Dark relation, 'You will have to take him to The Workhouse.'

Ada came out several times to the kitchen, still wiping out a bowl that was already clean and white. It was as though the wiping-out process gave her extra courage to fire at my Mother,

'You'me 'ard, our Nell, awful 'ard. He ain't doing no 'arm to nobody.'

'You feed and keep him then,' replied Mum sharply, 'You must think I keep a house for waifs and strays.'

The next Sunday, Dad brought an old overcoat and gave it to John.

'We're going for a walk,' he explained, and John followed without question.

The Workhouse was quite a distance away from our house. A whole district away in Fishponds, and then down a long lane called Challenge Hill. The Workhouse stood tall and forbidding, but all around that area was a beauty spot called Frenchay Glen. On high days and holidays we often set out for there. We took a bottle of lemonade made from yellow crystals which, when mixed with water made a refreshing drink. We had to pass The Workhouse and carry on down Blackberry Hill.

At the bridge at the bottom of the hill was a tiny iron turnstile, which you squeezed through and which brought you directly on to the river bank. A bit further on was a watermill. We always stopped by the watermill, fascinated by the volume of water that cascaded through and then splashed its way back down into the Frome again. Still further on, we came to a very fragile wooden bridge and lingered long on the rough boards looking down on the swift running water flowing in the stream below. It was just here, right by the side of overhanging boulders that the river formed a deep pool and it was here that we waded along the stony bottom and caught the tiddlers that darted out beneath the rocks in great shoals, and where once I had my plimsoles and socks pinched and I had to walk all the way home in bare feet.

Well, I tell you all this because it used to take us the best part of an hour to walk there. So it was with some surprise that John returned on that Sunday afternoon within half an hour and settled himself comfortably once more in the armchair by the fire.

'Where's Chas?' asked my Mother. There was no answer, only a cloud of smoke rose from the chair. Several hours later, my Father lifted the latch to the kitchen and peered round the door. He saw John sitting in the chair and my Mother looking at him for some explanation to it all.

'I lost him, ' he said at last, 'One minute he was right there beside me, next second he was gone.'

We all looked at John who smoked on contentedly,

'Ah,' was his only comment, 'Ah, that's how it were, ah.'

There were several more attempts to induce John to take the walk to The Workhouse before the successful venture eventually took place, and Dad returned looking forlorn and sad that it had been his lot to have to take his own brother there. Ada did another wailing willie bit which did not move my Mother an inch,

'Did you offer to feed him or wash for him?' she demanded. 'Then don't make me out to be the bad 'un of the piece.'

Every Sunday after that, my Father would go to see his brother and take him some tobacco and cakes that Mum had made. Even Ada would contribute a few pence towards the cost of this small treat. However, it all turned out quite well, because John suddenly took an interest in the garden and they gave him a little plot of his own to cultivate. We all took a turn to go and see him one sunny afternoon. We saw him bending over his flowers still puffing away at his smelly old pipe.

'I've brought you a root of Hester Reeds, and a few Pinks,' said Dad, 'I should put the pinks round the border, they'll make a nice show. Should put 'em in now if I were you.'

John straightened up and looked at Dad, then shifted his gaze to the ground again. "Ud 'ee now,' was all he said, "Ud 'ee now.'

18 · *Growing up*

Of all the spotty youths on the Patch, Stu Parker was the first to reach maturity. At fourteen, he was a good-looking but boastful lad who made no secret of his burning ambition to pursue every lass within reasonable running distance. Every night, up behind the bushes that had once been my beloved den, could be heard loud laughter from the lads and squeals of giggles from the girls, accompanied by scuffles and hushed voices. I was only dimly aware of a sexual secret being enacted, and whatever was going on did not meet with parental approval for suddenly there would be urgent calls of

'Come on home this instant, or you'll feel the strap across yer backside!'

There would be a general dispersing of the small knot of boys and girls with an irate parent yelling into the gathering darkness,

'Dirty little sod.'

Dad would bolt the gate and give a little grunt of satisfaction that all his women folk were safely in, and I would be toasting my knees by the big fire and reading *Peg's Paper*. The lurid tales in those pages were as unreal as the films we went to see, but they transported me to another world of mystery and romance. At thirteen, I was not remotely interested in boys, and sex was a word that belonged to marriage and courtship and that was a long way away. However, I was about to have my first lesson . . .

About six thirty the next evening, I was walking home the back way, when I was accosted by three girls who lived, not in our area, but from Halls Road which adjoined the lane at the far end. They surrounded me and whispered confidentially that I was urgently requested to hurry as there was something they all needed to know and only I could supply the answer. By this time I was deeply suspicious, but unable to escape. I was being hurried along with at least half a dozen girls on either side of me. We reached the den where Stu Parker and Jim Baker who lived next door to me were standing. Stu was by this time in long trousers, but Jim was still in short ones and his thin legs and bony knees looked slightly ridiculous as he lounged against the corrugated tin of Jackson's yard looking sheepish and laughing with embarrassment. Compared with Stu, Jim was a novice and it was apparent that whatever was about to take place, would be as raw and revealing to Jim as it would be for me. Stu was already unbuttoning his flies and thrust in his hand to produce his willie with a gesture of such admiration and pride. He stroked it, so that it seemed suddenly to come alive and grow bigger. With little gasps of wonder, the girls surged forward and leaned over to touch the quivering thing, and then withdraw with little shrieks of pure delight. All the time, Jim who should have been following suit and displaying his talent to the world, was rolling over and over against the fence almost doubled up with laughter. When he finally collapsed onto the ground helpless with mirth, I went to help him up and began to laugh, too. I gave one final glance towards Stu, whose eyes appeared to have rolled backwards into his head in sheer ecstasy as all these fingers and shrieks sent him some place between the den and the top of Jackson's furnace, and clutched at Jim, weeping with hysterical mirth.

Then I heard Jim's sister calling him in a two-syllable and strident voice,

'Jim-my come away from that dirty little sod.'

I pulled Jim to his feet and still laughing, we ran down the lane to arrive at his house with flushed faces — a sign Jim's sister must have taken for guilt, because she boxed his ears and pushed him all the way up the path calling over her shoulder at me,

'Does your father know what you've been up to, you hussy?' I didn't say a word, not even when Mum looked at me enquiringly when she saw my flushed face and said,

'What've you bin up to?'

I didn't say a word. I was too scared. But there were a thousand questions I wanted to ask. They were all forgotton the next day, though, because Dad took me for a ride and showed me a scene I have never forgotten.

Of all the memories I count as happiest in those growing up years, were the ones spent with Dad when we would drag our bikes from the shed and start off on a voyage of discovery.

That year 1930 was another bad one, not only for us, but for everyone. It was the time that Dad was laid off at Jackson's, and he looked ill and worried as he travelled from place to place on that upright, heavy bike of his, trying to get employment at other local firms. When he arrived home at the end of the day, his face was white and strained. There would be no word exchanged between Mum and Dad, apart from a momentary enquiring glance, she would resume her machining with just a tired and resigned sigh.

The Wall Street Crash in America had plunged the world into recession. The Great Depression, it was called, and it was from America that we got songs like 'Buddy, can you spare a dime?' and the dole queues everywhere got longer. Prohibition in America also brought a spate of films about gangland and stars like Edward G. Robinson as Al Capone filled our screens.

On those precious weekends, I would be Dad's constant companion on long rides into the country. Dad was not a conversationalist, and we would ride for long periods without a word being spoken. Yet I knew that these quiet spells were necessary for him, and although he didn't talk, he was acutely aware of what was happening around him. My safety and welfare were of prime importance to him; he helped to shape my values and like him, come to absorb the countryside and to cherish a deep love for it. He had an inner strength and the ability to see, to understand and to care deeply. He could not express the things he saw or felt. Even to write was difficult and painful for him and my Mother did all the correspondence and handled all the money.

It was February, and there had been a slight fall of snow. The hedges looked as though they had been covered in a thin layer of cotton wool. Already a thaw had set in, a thin watery sun had melted the snow and occasionally the heavy branches overhead would suddenly be loosed of their burden and the snow would slip, and fall to the ground in a white flurry. A small Robin, sheltering in the hedge, would show its redbreast, peep out startled by the avalanche, and then shaking its wings, would fly away. In fact, there was quite a chorus of birdsong on that late February morning as Dad and I bowled along, and the air held a promise of Spring, and the twittering of the birds and the barking of dogs was like a sudden awakening of something exciting about to happen.

Only a milk cart, with the clink of the metal urn and the cheery whistle of the milkman, and the shrill sound of a bicycle bell disturbed the silence as we rode along the road, with the wind making a humming sound as it blew through the coloured strands of cord that protected the mudguard of my bike. When we freewheeled down a hill, with my father in front showing me by example always the need for caution, the cold wind blew and screamed through my hair and into my ears. But the mad acceleration would finally slacken and leave me with wind-whipped cheeks, and almost breathless I would laugh out loud as I caught Dad's expression, for his eyes would be shining too. It was as though there was a sudden extra blaze of light that brightened his face to know I was sharing his love and delight.

There was one other secret that we shared, yet never spoke about. An unwritten law prevented it. I took the place of his beloved Nell. She was the one who should have been by his side, and as the years passed and I grew to look more like my Mother, he took pleasure in watching me as though I perpetuated a dream that he had never realised in life, but played out in fantasy with me. As far back as that crisp February morning I realised that the love he held for me was born from a longing that he had for my Mother, and because I so deperately wanted to reach out for love myself, I was deeply conscious of the lack of affection that was his cross to bear as well.

That morning, we pushed our bikes up a winding lane, and stopped for a while beside a wooden gate shaped into an arch. It led into a garden that was walled with grey stone. The gate was partly open and out of sheer curiosity, Dad pushed it open and then stood there transfixed. He stood aside so that I, too, could have a peep and what I saw I shall never forget. By the side of a pond, and growing all around the edge, were masses and masses of pure white snowdrops with drooping flower heads like great pearl drops nodding slightly in the wind. As we peeped through the half-open gate, a whirl of wings rose from the lawn beyond the pond, as tiny birds fluttered to the safety of the ivy-clad wall, where they set up such a twittering that it was almost as if they were protesting vigorously against this un-welcome intrusion into their privacy. Whilst we stood in silent admiration and awe at the lovely sight, one small bird flew from the shelter of the leaves and perched on the edge of the embroidered white border of the pond, until, emboldened by the long interval of silence, others hopped to join him in tentative little leaps and calling to each other with shrill high notes. The birds flew down again amongst the snowdrops, under the trees and across the lawn, talking to each other in easy familiarity, a kind of family squabbling that filled the air with a delicious sense of peace and understanding that even here, territory was held as dear and necessary as we rush to the warmth and security of our land and home.

We both stood for a long time deep in our own thoughts. Dad with his hands in his pockets and his blue eyes smiling. Then he gave a contented sigh, and we tiptoed out softly, almost reverently closing the gate behind us.

19 · *A Bereavement*

In 1930 Aunt Flo died. Aunt Flo the peacemaker. When Ada battled with my Mother, and her wild blue eyes showered fiery red darts into Mum's calm brown ones, it was Flo who would come quietly up behind her sister and lead her back to the front parlour. Aunt Flo who took the never-ending sixpence from her savings jar at Christmas to buy us both the bumper writing pad in which to scribble, and the glossy Tiger Tim annuals that cost a whole half-crown and seemed such a colossal amount. It was Aunt Flo who had bought me the book *Ann of Green Gables*, and on the fly-leaf had written,

'When I am dead and in my grave, and all my bones are rotten, Take up this book, and think of me, when I am all forgotten.'

A few months prior to her death I had been in a state of mad rebellion, for I was turned out of the tiny back bedroom which I had thought of as mine, permanent and secure, to change places with brother Dennis. The calm had been shattered one bright morning by Mother declaring that,

'It's disgusting!'

Just what was so disgusting was soon to be revealed, for when I slipped into the kitchen, a battle royal was being waged about the fact that Dennis, who was fast approaching fourteen, was still sleeping in the big front room with the two Aunts. This situation was dealt with promptly and without delay, although not exactly to the satisfaction of all concerned. For once, Ada and Flo accepted the cold fact that Mum was right, and looked suitably mollified and modest enough to concede to the impending change-over. I seethed with bitterness and resentment all the while my single iron bedstead was being removed to its new position alongside the side window of the front room. After that, there was barely enough room to move. I had only the small three-drawer chest that was to house my treasured possessions, and a large wooden screen dividing me from the rest of the room plus a round peg mat by the side of the bed.

Dennis never made a comment about his removal to his new surroundings. It would appear that because of his placid nature, he was beloved, nurtured and cherished, and things just fell into his lap without effort. I was a different matter. In my own jaundiced view, even the things I fought for, loved, and believed in, could all be wrested from me. I would lie in my bed at night, my mind festering with dark thoughts.

One morning, something awakened me very early and opening my eyes, and still heavy with sleep, I saw a bird fly through the window and straight at me. I cried out at the swiftness of it, and put up my hand to cover my face and to ward it off. When I looked again, the bird was no longer there. I began to wonder if I had dreamed it all. The impression had been so real that even to this day can recall it vividly. This time, when I recounted the incident to my Mother, she actually stopped drinking her tea to look at me and say, 'Birds are a sign of death.'

Flo had been working at Douglas's for some time now, cleaning the shiny new bikes for when they went on show. She used to bring home piles of tiny alloy discs which we used as imitation money when we played shops or post office. I was not aware, either then or now, just how the discs were created, or of the exact nature of her work, but Ada said FIo often worked with her hands in some kind of paraffin or spirit. One day she came home to show Mum a strange rash that had appeared on her hands and face and neck. She also had some difficulty in breathing. When I lay awake at night, I could hear her laboured breath and it made me feel I couldn't breathe either. Finally the doctor came and said she had congestion of the lungs, and recommended that a steam kettle should be used to ease her breathing.

The kettle was bought and with the steady hiss that released the steam from the long spout, there also came the strangled gasp of long-drawn-out breaths that ended in a kind of troubled sigh, a noise that scared me, and filled me with an urgent sense to do something for her, though I knew she was already beyond any human aid or skill. That Sunday afternoon, the Salvation Army formed a little knot of people in red bonnets and caps, just below the window of our house and the band struck up a tune,

'Come ye sinners, come to Jesus.'

The man on the drum thumped away whilst Mum hurried out to ask them if they wouldn't mind moving further on down the street, because there was someone very ill upstairs. One of the brothers immediately offered to come in and offer up a prayer, but when he stood at the bedroom door twisting his peaked cap nervously in his hand, Aunt Flo opened bright feverish eyes full on him and said in a weak, almost inaudible voice,

'Tain't prayin' I needs, but the doctor.'

Aunt Flo died that night propped up against my

Mother who was cradling her in her arms. She was protesting feebly that she didn't want to die for who would take care of Ada? Then she gave out a long drawn-out raspy breath that sounded like the air being expelled from a balloon and lay very still. Mum said that she had died and that night I slept with my brother Dennis and we cried ourselves to sleep. Dennis from a genuine sense of loss, and me from fear and a knowledge of death that I had not experienced before.

The following morning, Ada's eyes were both red and wild. She would appear in our kitchen with tears falling like large copious dew-drops that ran down her face in a never-ending stream. Dad led her gently to his big wooden chair where she sat numbly staring at us in a pathetic, vacant sort of way. The day of the funeral was the day we dreaded most, but Ada did not ask to see her sister buried. She sat quietly and stony-faced in the chair by the fire, staring at the bare brick wall of the house next door that made our kitchen as dark and grim as perhaps her thoughts were.

Towards evening, she made a move to get up to go somewhere. My Father, still anxious for her, enquired if he could help in some way.

'I'm going to Flo.' she said, 'I'm going to dig 'er up.'

I stood there whilst her gaze shifted to mine. She said, 'I wish I were like your Jayce. She's strong. She'll get by no matter what the odds.'

She went to push past me, but I held her hand, for somehow I could identify with that desperate feeling that I knew was so agonising for her. Then I was holding her hands and gently rubbing them and pulling her back to the chair and easing her neck until she relaxed and was crying softly but not hysterically like before, and the tears that flowed were healing tears that unwound the tension and scars of grief. I knew, because I had buried my tears of grief all those years ago.

'I wish I was like you,' she said again at last, but this time there was no bitterness, spite or malice in her voice. It came out in a dead, flat sort of way.

20 · *A Romance*

After the death of Aunt Flo, Ada became less aggressive. She was always ready to 'have a go' in a verbal battle, and her large blue staring eyes still spat fire and brimstone at my Mother. However, the long steady stare that Mum returned immediately made Ada retreat to the safety of the door, still incessantly wiping out the already spotlessly clean bowl. It was now Denny who would emerge from the front room to act as her protector and to lead her gently back there.

One evening, just after tea, Ada came through the sitting room door and into the kitchen. I was startled to see her face covered in powder and it looked as though she had sprinkled the flour dredger all over it. Her apron had been discarded and a new green crepe dress with yellow flowers down the front had been donned. She reeked of cologne as though the contents of the bottle had been splashed on too liberally.

My Mother regarded her enquiringly. Ada stopped and demanded:

'Well?'

'Where's the fire? Have you seen your face?'

Ada wiped at her face and then muttered that it was none of Mum's business. At that moment, Denny emerged armed with a toothbrush and commenced battle with his teeth over the kitchen sink.

'It would be nice,' my Mother said in exasperation. 'To finish my tea for once, without the healthy gum routine.'

Ada took a deep breath and stuck out her chest like a battleship in full sail, but before she had a chance to say anything, Denny gathered his toothbrush, soap and towel, joined forces with her and together they swept from the room — leaving my Mother fuming over the intrusion and the insolence that amounted to contempt.

Later that evening, we heard a loud knock on the front

door. We also heard Aunt Ada's voice and the much deeper tones of a man. Then the front room door closed and despite the number of times tiptoed to the door, all I heard was low and subdued voices. At precisely ten o'clock we heard the front door open and close, then silence once more.

It soon became evident that Ada was entertaining a male visitor. Twice a week the heavy scent of perfume would proceed the flour-white face. The gentle tap at the door and the low conversation would continue until the stroke of ten. Sometimes Ada would creep into the kitchen with a supercilious grin on her tight thin lips, but the crepe dress would be gone and in its place, the old familiar skirt and jumper covered with the flowered apron.

'My God! She's got a man,' exclaimed my Father, 'Who would have guessed it?'

'Love is blind, but a bloke must be blind to fall for a face like that,' Mum said unkindly.

Several months later, Ada sailed triumphantly into the kitchen. It was a meal time of course. She announced to a stunned audience that she was getting married and Frank, her man friend wanted to discuss a few business items with my parents. My Father quickly removed the milk bottle from the table, got some clean cups from the dresser and proceeded to mash a fresh pot of tea. We hardly had time to tidy round before the figure of Frank burst upon us. Dad shoo'd the cat from the only comfortable chair in the room and Frank took the seat, obviously very much at ease.

He said he was Steward of the Conservative Club at St. George. He smoked a lot, for his fingers were stained with nicotine, and his hands shook slightly. He looked then and indeed, always, slightly inebriated and wore the perpetual grin of beer-soaked intelligence. Periodically, he would bang his forehead with the flat of his hand, as though he had forgotten something, and finally he stammered out that he was intending to marry Ada and whisk her away. He had thought it all out. She was a good worker and she would keep the bar and premises at the club clean. Added to that, he had seen how well she looked after Dennis, and he was confident she would supply his every need as well. He thought that she must have been married before, as she had this one son — but when she had been asked, she would not give him any information. He wondered if my Mother could shed any light on this question, but my Mother declined to answer. She told him,

'You know as much as I do. She has never been the one to spill any gossip or family secrets.'

Frank was clearly disappointed and slightly embarrassed, but as he rose unsteadily to depart, he said he would merely state in passing, as he had a house in Birchells Green Avenue, he would not be thinking of settling here. Dennis, of course, would be going with them.

My Mother, tight-lipped and silent, said goodnight without getting up to see him to the door. Ada came through to the kitchen confident and triumphant. Mother almost leapt at her,

'The boy stays here,' she said emphatically, 'He is my son.'

'He comes with me,' Ada replied, standing her ground and looking defiant. Her two blue eyes glinted madly, and levelled themselves directly at my Mother as she almost hissed out the words, 'He is mine and he comes with me.'

The bowl was still vigorously being wiped out when my brother Dennis appeared on the scene. He was very white and shaking and he said with obvious emotion,

'I shall go with Ada and Frank. I have had enough of the rows and bothers in this house over me. I want some peace away from the lot of you.'

He then took Ada by the arm and they walked into the front room and closed the door. A fortnight later, they moved out and a strange silence fell on the house.

Nobody went to the wedding, which was a quiet Registry Office affair. I moved into my parents' old room, and the front bedroom was for the very first time occupied by my parents. All the years that I had contrived to enter the front parlour by kicking on the door or screaming blue murder on the stairs were over. I could go in or out at will. But the room never appealed to me again, and the ghosts of the two Aunts haunted it then as they still do today.

My Mother often stopped her machining to cry. Large tears would roll down her cheeks and when she spoke to a neighbour she would sob uncontrollably that she would never see her son again. I was amazed and startled, for never once had my brother exchanged more than a few brief words in passing, and she had never whole-heartedly enforced her demand that he should be with her and the family. I wanted to reach out to tell her that I wanted her love, and there was Dad as well who would have done anything just for a sign of interest or concern. Once more I was on the outside struggling for attention that would have made all the difference in the world, but as the days went by I began almost to hate my brother for the virtues she suddenly bestowed upon him. Dennis did things so much better than I could ever hope to do; his handwriting was a joy to read, whilst mine was a spidery scrawl with inkblots everywhere; he could spell, I could not; Den tackled things in a quiet, methodical way, I was untidy and tore things up if they didn't come right first time. Dennis had never been any trouble. He had never had a day's illness in his life. That was why the two Aunts had loved him and fussed over him, and she had been glad of their help because of all the trouble I had been.

She went out one day and did not return until tea-time. I overheard her telling Ma Saunders that she had been to a fortune-teller to ask if Dennis would ever return. She had been told that he would return suddenly and be extremely sorry for the sorrow he had caused. I blurted out in anger,

'He will come back when he wants something, all right. But the sorrow bit is what you want to hear, he doesn't feel anything. He only knows what he wants.'

She turned on me then in spite and anger.

'Don't you talk about your brother and his feelings, you had none for me when you returned from Painswick.'

I felt suddenly sick for there was a growing antagonism between us that developed in intensity every day. As I grew more like my Mother in looks, it seemed the attention my Father gave me infuriated her, and the days I spent riding with him, he often seemed remote and far away. I was apart from him and apart from her and felt lonely, cut off and sad. Sad, because I was confused and unable to understand what was happening and certainly completely at a loss to know what to do.

21 · *Housewifery*

In our last year at school, we had what used to be called Housewifery Classes. About six of us would walk across the playground to Mr. Webley the Caretaker, and he used to escort us in a file to a flat next door to his own. He opened the door with a key taken from a huge bunch which hung from his belt. Inside the flat was a sitting room, kitchen, bedroom and toilet. There was a doll in a pram and there was a tin bath. We had a rota of cleaning jobs we had to complete to learn how to keep house, and we had to dust and sweep and polish. The baby had to be changed and bathed and rocked to sleep.

Usually though, as soon as the door closed upon us, we would bounce on the bed and shriek with laughter, tell each other jokes or play hide-and-seek in all the rooms. Over endless cups of tea we'd bring out our 'penny dreadfuls' and read the spicy bits to one another. As for the baby — it fared dreadfully, often being upended and its head stuck in the potty, whilst Gladys did the 'splits' with her dress tucked into her knickers for decency.

One of us always stayed on guard for the surprise visit of a teacher so that we were never caught out. And by the time she swept in, we were models of good behaviour, industriously polishing the already gleaming furniture or washing the always spotless floor.

We all had to bring ingredients for the meal, which we took turns in cooking, and parents grumbled regularly about this unnecessary extravagance, no doubt reasoning that a great girl of thirteen would have learned all this at home, anyway. As for us, we enjoyed these excursions to the flat enormously. It was a change from the severe discipline of the classroom and none of us took the domestic side of it seriously. It was a welcome break; and if its real purpose was to prepare us for the hard and often drab reality of the real world outside the school gates, we were simply not ready for it.

Looking back, it seems amazing to me how ignorant we were. It's so difficult to describe in today's climate of freedom. But we were, for example, woefully ignorant of sexual matters. Nobody told us anything. Grown-ups suffered from crippling shyness in discussing anything 'in front of the children'. There were half-embarrassed, half-giggling references to the Stork or being found under a gooseberry bush. But people were not only very Victorian in their attitudes, but as I realise now, incredibly ignorant about the workings of their own bodies. Small wonder then, that in answer to my anxious question, my Mother would often shake her head and sniff,

'You'll find out soon enough, my girl.'

So, I knew nothing of the great secret of how babies happened. We girls whispered together in that flat, sharing grossly inaccurate information and nothing that I heard persuaded me in favour of marriage or being a wife and mother. Rather the reverse. And what I did

97

know, what I had already found out appalled me. All my uncles were often the worse for drink and sexually and physically abused their wives. The women in our family often wore cowed and care-worn look of the constantly afraid — except that is, for my own Mother. My Dad never hit any us, but then he was seen as being 'weak'!

If it got to the point where a woman couldn't stand it any more, there was nowhere for her to go. The woman who left her husband and went back to her Mother was sharply told,

'You made your bed, now you must lie on it.'

And Father would say,

'No man must interfere between man and wife,' and pack his errant daughter off home again.

And if an unmarried girl got into trouble, she was a bad girl. She got a thrashing from her father and if the man would not marry her, she was often sent away to a Home. Most women would feel a kind of sympathy for her and you would often hear the comment,

'Poor little bitch.'

But they could do nothing constructive, and she would be pointed out in the street as a kind of horrible example and her shame perpetuated.

So I think it was a kind of act of rebellion that we put the doll's head in the pee-pot. We all knew that there was some sort of inevitability about our lives that we couldn't avoid, so that hanging on to this innocence was a memory we would cherish forever. The days when we giggled over silly things and life held no responsibility, no drudgery, when the days were long and the sun shone were to be spun out as long as possible.

We were aware of our parent's struggle, but we hoped with youthful optimism that their lot would not be ours; by this simple act of defiance we were saying that we would not tolerate what they accepted without question. Reading trashy stories about girls who married rich men was an escape from harsh reality. Even the films transported us into a realm of fantasy and held us spellbound with stories of the poor girl who married the millionaire. When dreamed and sighed and told my mother I would only marry a rich man so that I could have my wall-to-wall carpets and my red velvet curtains, she would reply, with a curl of her lips and almost with contempt,

'Don't get ideas above your station, my girl. Just remember you are nothing and what you read in books or see in films never happens in real life.'

22 · *My First Job*

It was a day like any other day when I walked for the last time out of the playground of Two Mile Hill Girls' School in 1931. No friends milled around me to wish me luck as I now ventured into the frightening world of adult life. My fourteenth birthday had coincided with the end of term holidays.

Everybody was eager for the six weeks break. Six of us had been handed a long brown envelope, and once outside, I ripped it open to read my mind-shattering school testimonial. This precious slip of paper would go with me on every job I ever wrote or answered an advertisement for. I glanced down at Miss Duggan's sprawling handwriting; on a twelve inch square piece of vellum paper it stated simply:

'This is to certify that Beryl Joyce Dark has been a pupil of this school for the past seven years. Having reached the accepted standard her general work is good. Her regularity is good. Her conduct is good. She is clean and neat in appearance. She is honest and truthful.'

Not much, I thought bitterly, to be armed with out there in that big world and the great work force that I was about to become part of. I guessed that the ability to rise and shine at some unearthly hour and to be able to clock in on the dot was far more important than any academic qualification.

Before coming out into the freedom and sunshine, I had taken one last look around the hall. I noted the Honours Boards with the names of girls who had won scholarships, their names emblazoned for all to see in letters of gold. From the whole school perhaps only one would be fortunate to gain the coveted place, and for a whole year she would be placed on a pedestal as a shining example of what we could all achieve through the gracious auspices of our wonderful educational system which was the best in the world.

I had made no such mark of distinction. Little Miss Average I, along with a million other Miss Averages. No one would ever know that we had ever been inside those walls. Miss Dugdale's desk stood on a raised wooden platform in the recess by the window, enforcing the impression that this was the 'Head' and let everybody bend the knee. The very name commanded respect. The cane, symbol of discipline hung in front of the desk for all to see and mark well. The Punishment and Reward system never failed. You behaved yourself or else. I often felt the swish of the cane hurtling down on my defence-less palm. The sting came later when my palm smarted for hours along with dark thoughts that never quite eradicated the fear.

I stopped only once more at the forge at the top of the lane where old Tom Pillinger was making the sparks fly and I listened to the chink of hammer on steel as he shoed a horse. Now no more would stand fascinated and silent as the horse stood patiently waiting for her new shoes. The stopping and the running on to the school was part of a very intimate school scene; it was as important as the four red indian eyes you got at the tuck shop for a ha'penny. I felt tearful and sad, tossed about with emotions I didn't understand and couldn't cope with. At fourteen I didn't feel grown up and what was more, I didn't want to.

100

On the following Tuesday morning, my Mother informed me that Lottie Collins, who kept a drapery store next door to Williams the vegetable shop, wanted to see me. She had told my Mother when she had popped in there for half a yard of reversible cretonne at 6¾ pence a yard, that she knew of a job that would be 'just right for your Joyce' and I was to go down to see her right away.

The Collins's were respected business people in Kingswood. Old man Collins had a grocery store and was astute enough to know that if he gave good service to his customers he was looking after his own bread and butter. He had four children; three girls all in drapery shops scattered about the city, and a son. This son was now married with a small child and was about to set up in business in a modest little shop in Bedminster along the Cut. This I discovered, was where I came in.

Lottie made a lot about the job, glossing it over so that it sounded like the chance of a lifetime. I was to receive FIVE WHOLE SHILLINGS a week. She mentioned the five bob first. She was quite right — I had never had five bob in the whole of my life. Once Uncle (who was blind) had given me a half sovereign in mistake for a shilling. My Mother had covered my hand with hers and held it tight; afterwards she had offered me two shillings for the half sovereign and I had joyfully accepted.

My duties would be simple, she had said, merely helping in the house with a bit of cleaning and light cooking. There was the little girl to be fetched from school but I would be very happy there — she just knew that I would get on with her brother Harold, and of course I would get good food. The best.

My Mother made me a blue velvet holdall with brown bone handles. She also made me a flannelette nightie and a skirt with two warm blouses. I started my duties the following Monday.

Harold Collins was tall and freckly, he had a boyish face and pleasing manner. Like his father, he respected

101

his customers and wished only to do the best he could by them. His wife was different. She also was tall and slim but with a haughty manner. She looked down on me now, and although her smile was as bright as a 60-watt lamp, I could tell she was thinking — could this slip of a girl with the dark brown eyes and mass of curly hair get through the rota of duties she had in mind for her. She quickly made a decision and spoke to me.

'I shall require you to help with the preparation of the meals, the washing-up and clearing away. I am much too busy helping my husband with the business. There will, of course, be a certain amount of cleaning to be done and I shall allocate your various duties daily. I have a daughter who will need to be fetched from school and you will be required to play with her until bedtime. There will be a small amount of mending and sewing to be done, but shall we give it a try say for a week? See how we get on?'

She then showed me a little box room which contained a bed and a small bedside cabinet, but outside on the landing was a cupboard which she said I could use to hang my things, and a shelf above was also at my disposal. The cupboard had a musty smell.

I found nothing hard or difficult in the work I had to do in the days that followed. I loved the child and read and played with her for hours. Only one thing worried me. I came down one morning to find that she had put a duck board down for me to stand on to start the washing. The big tub stood on a long bench. Even with the duck board, I could hardly see over the top, and the heat and steam made me feel hot and faint. At home, I might have helped to turn the mangle but I had never actually done the washing. It was all done by hand, sheets; tablecloths, shirts, overalls, the lot. That night I fell into bed sick with exhaustion.

Every Thursday afternoon from two to eight-thirty was my 'half day'. I sometimes walked along the river bank and then had tea in a cafe somewhere feeling very lonely but grown up and quite a woman of the world. One day I took a walk down Castle Street and then I saw it, a coat with a fur collar that would make me look like a film star. The more I looked at it, the more convinced I became that must have it. I hardly needed the shop walker to convince me that she was sure that if I came inside there would be something to suit 'Modom'. I said I wanted to try on the coat in the window. She said she was sorry but they did not take things from the window until the window was due to be dressed. I was not going to be put off that coat.

'Fetch the manager,' I said curtly.

She looked very frightened at that, but he came. A short, dapper little man in pin-striped trousers and a thin Ronald Coleman moustache. Everybody sprouted Ronald Coleman smackers about that time. He confirmed what the shop walker had said, almost as if they were in league with each other.

In the end, it was agreed that I should go on paying for the coat and as soon as the last instalment was paid, and the window redressed, it would be packed and my name put on the box ready for me to collect. Every Thursday after that, I religiously went to the shop and paid my five shillings off the £2.10s. coat. One more payment only now remained and this Thursday I would be collecting it.

I skipped the bedrooms, I sang as I flipped the duster lightly over the ornaments. The vegetables were ready and standing in salted water and the meat was already in the large meat tin surrounded by the potatoes that were to be baked for supper. Lunch was cold meat and salad which I intended to miss because of wanting to be out on the dot. It was just ten minutes to two when, in my best black stockings and grey jersey coat I presented myself for my wages.

Mrs. Collins hesitated, then looked at her watch. As if to reassure herself that she was absolutely sure of the time, she glanced up at the big clock on the wall. Under my breath I said 'damn!' I should have waited until dead on two.

'Ah now,' she said and my heart sank. 'There is a small job I would like you to do before you go. It shouldn't take long and then I will have your money ready for you and you can be away. Now there is no need to be too fussy, but I would like the coal cellar washed over. Put the house flannel on the end of the broom but give it a good brush first.'

It never occurred to me to refuse her. I just stood there in abject misery knowing it would mean having to take off all my best clothes, then afterwards I would have to wash before I could go out. It would be three o'clock before I would be out of the house on my precious half day.

I suddenly became very angry and a red mist swam before my eyes. I would wash her bloody floor like it had never been washed before. To this day I can never remember getting the pail or the water, but I began to scrub each patch slowly and methodically. I didn't feel the stone floor tear and ladder the only pair of black silk stockings I possessed. The adrenalin poured into my blood-stream giving me all the energy I needed. My face was smudged with coaldust and tears, my black dress, where the water had dripped onto the front, was stained and filthy. It was only when I came to the final patch did I then look up and swore a terrible oath.

'God or the Devil,' I said quietly, 'This is the last time in my entire bloody life I will ever do anyone's housework. Never again will I be on my knees with my nose to the ground, for I belong up there with my eyes to the light and walking upright and tall.'

I emptied the pail and washed it clean with cold water. I washed the scrubbing brush and the house flannel and putting both in the bottom of the pail, I climbed the cellar steps and quietly put the pail away for the last time. I picked up my coat from the peg where I had hung it before that last wild rage had overtaken me, and walked upstairs.

Mrs. Collins opened her mouth to say something when she saw the state I was in, but took a step backward when she also saw the wild glint in my eyes that held the clear message that our paths would never meet again. She held out my five shillings to me as though I were a leper that she had no intention of touching. I passed her without a word. There was just one more thing I had to do. I ran upstairs to collect the blue velvet holdall that my Mother had made for me just ten short weeks ago. I had worked blindly and solidly for this woman for ten weeks, for a coat I was now going to collect come hell or high water.

I must have looked a sight with my coal-black face, my stockings all torn and my hair dishevelled, and with that dreadful determined look on my face. Even the shop walker ran to collect the coat when demanded to have it now and not a moment later.

I never saw the long stares of the passers-by or the passengers as sat huddled in the corner of the tram car on its way back to Kingswood.

When I opened the door of the sitting-room, my Mother was still on the machine. She looked up, but suddenly stopped when she saw my face and the utter misery and dejection so clearly there. She watched me fling myself into a chair and sob. Hard sobs that tore at my insides and made it difficult to breath. She waited until I had quietened down, then with a long sigh she said,

'I'll go and make us a nice cup of tea, girl.'

23 · The Corset Factory

It was Elsie who once again came to my rescue and took the coat to renovate completely. She told me I must never buy a coat with a big fur collar, because only tall girls with long, elegant necks could effectively wear them. Little

Joyce at 15 or 16 years old in hand-me-down sateen dress

shorties like me had to be content with a tiny band for a collar and wear boxy jackets. I received this news with downcast heart, for I had dreamed of this great fur collar ever since I had seen the huge fur collars of my heroines on the screen. However, Elsie went off to buy several yards of astrakhan and this she sewed around the neck and all down the front of the coat, and around the bottom as well. The bottom was a flared skirt which she shortened, and the end result was a replica of a skating outfit. She made a small fur hat from the collar, and I also had a muff. When it was completed, I looked a treat and had stares of envy from the other girls. When they were catty, I just knew they were green with jealousy and I would toss my curls and feel good.

Elsie also found me my first real job. She did what my Mother did not. At the local corset factory called Langridge's, she personally knew the mangeress, Miss Joy. More formally, her name was Mrs. Blackford and both she and her husband worked for Mr. Ryall and his son, Charlie, who owned the family concern. Elsie always went to Miss Joy to be measured for her corsets. For these, she paid a sum of money that made my Mother gasp, for she would never be able to afford such luxury, and had to wait until Elsie finished with her old ones and handed them over to her.

Elsie enquired from Miss Joy whether any vacancies existed and mentioned me. Miss Joy promised an interview but nothing else. The following week, I received a letter — I was to call at the offices in Waters Road and ask for Rebe Fudge.

My first glimpse of the inside of a corset factory filled me with fear and trepidation. The noise of the machines, all whirring incessantly, and the white-aproned girls with arms full of half-finished garments, and other girls bent low over the machines, hardly daring to lift their eyes for fear of losing precious seconds in piece-time rates, dismayed and appalled me. I was led through the workshop and into a tiny office at the far end where Miss Joy was deep in conversation with a young man from the cutting department. Miss Joy was red-faced, with grey hair that was strained back from her face and wound in a bun at the nape of her neck. She looked severe and her thin lips did nothing to soften the contour of her face. She invited me to sit and scooped a large pile of cloth from the chair to allow me to do so. The young man from the cutting department eyed me for a few seconds, then with an audacious wink at me, he left the room and we were left alone. Miss Joy eyed me for some time, then shot a question at me, 'Have you ever used a machine before? We use electric machines here.'

'No,' I said simply, 'I have not.'

She leaned towards me, and touched my hair admiringly. For a second it seemed that the mouth would soften into a smile, but in the next breath she said quickly, 'You will be required to put up your hair and wear a protective cap.' murmured something inaudible, and she sat there in deep thought for what seemed like an interminable time. Finally, she seemed to make up her mind, for she said briskly,

'Follow me!'

We came out of the building and into a kind of warehouse situated on the opposite side of the road. We went up a flight of stairs and entered a packing room which was a hive of activity, but without the incessant noise of the machines. A happy babble of voices was going on all around us and although the pace of work never faltered, I was much more comfortable here than in the factory which we had just left. Down the centre of the room sat about twenty or thirty girls snipping at thread ends on the corsets. With nimble fingers they twisted and turned the finished garment, which was then collected by a foremistress and put into a pile where three pressers skillfully pressed a cool iron along the creases and then piled the finished corsets onto a table. Another girl then sorted the piles into sizes and checked the numbers against the final order. Finally, three more girls took the completed piles, rolled them in soft paper and put them into boxes. The girls at the end tied up the boxes and marked each one with the appropriate size.

I was handed over to Phillis Baxter who was in charge of the girls. was introduced to Mr. Woolrich who was foreman of the packing department. Everybody stared and I felt awkward and strange until a pretty girl called Barbara stepped forward and began to show me how to fold some Tea Rose brassieres and put them into bags. Later that afternoon, I was given a long green overall and cap, and Mr. Woolrich handed me a red note-book in which he had to insert the hours per week that I worked. He also informed me that I would be starting on one penny three farthings an hour for a forty eight hour week, with a rise of one farthing an hour every six months. So now I had really joined the ranks of the great working class. I went to work at seven thirty each morning, and worked until six or six thirty each evening. By the time I rushed home and had my tea there wasn't much of the day to relax in. Yet we found time to go to the pictures, to visit friends and go dancing. On Saturdays, we caught the tram and went into Old Market Street where the stalls and the barrow boys shouted their wares, and for one and threepence you could have three pictures taken by a photographer called Jerome, or we could call in at Lyons Corner tea shop in Castle Street and to the clatter of tea cups and the happy chatter of people, while away an hour over a cuppa that cost no more than three half pence. Yes, I was happy then. The years that lay ahead were full of promise. I was young, I had a job. Life was as good as I could reasonably expect it to be. But not for long.

24 · *Patrick*

Mrs. Baker, our next door neighbour, had a new lodger. We had both noticed him, my Mother and I, when we were hanging out the washing. He opened their gate and glanced our way over the three foot wall that divided the houses. I know that I had stared because he was outstandingly different from the men I had seen around Kingswood. When he spoke to my Mother and raised his hat, my Mother giggled and dropped all the pegs in the peg bag. He was in uniform when we had first caught sight of him; a sergeant walking stiff and upright, as though he were still on the parade ground, with his cap well down over his eyes, and carrying his cane under his arm. We were all-atwitter to find out about him, and Mrs. Denton told us he was her oldest son's sergeant who was retired from the Army now, but was staying with them until he could look round to see what he wanted to do. His name was Patrick O'Hara and he was indeed Irish. The second sight of him confirmed it. He was in his early forties, his black hair only sprinkled with grey hair around the temples served to give him an attractive and distinguished air. The eyes were blue and roguish and when he laughed, as he often did, they danced and shone and crinkled at the corners. He did a little tap dance, and I had the impression that he was always about to whisk you up and dance away with you. That Saturday morning, he had actually stopped and leaned over the wall to speak to us. Although he was speaking to my Mother, he kept looking at me and I became amused when she at length asked me to run indoors and pop the potatoes on for dinner. Clearly, she was impressed with him.

As the days passed, he became a popular and familiar figure, especially with the kids on The Patch. He would give the younger ones a ride on his bike when they saw him riding down the lane. Sometimes he would stand outside the gate and invite the boys to test his strength by holding out his arm and letting the boys swing on it. Every so often, he would go into his little dance routine. I also noticed that my Mother would often get up from her machine and stroll down towards the open gate and watch with interest at his exploits. Then he would casually walk towards my Mother and engage her in conversation, but always looking down at his feet, finding something very amusing there. Once, when I was coming down the lane, he pulled up beside me and I was laughing about a silly little incident that had just happened and which secretly amused me. He stopped right there in the lane and looked intently at me. There was nobody in the lane, and I felt uncomfortable with him looking at me so hard that his eyes seemed to flash. I made the excuse that I had heard my Mother call, waved to him and ran quickly into the house. Mum glanced up quickly as I came in and her look was hostile, especially when she heard the Bakers' gate open and close at that precise moment. I felt guilty and angry at the same time, but nothing was said and I was glad to have my dinner and get back to work.

The following Saturday, I noticed Mum wearing a new dress in green flowered silk. She was always neatly dressed and she could run up anything on that old treadle. Yet it was mostly skirts and blouses that I saw her in. The green silk suited her and her dark brown eyes and dark hair with the green velvet band made me realise how attractive she was. She had strong off-white teeth, when she smiled they showed wide and even. Although she was neither tall and elegant nor small and petite, she had a motherly, matronly appeal which you could not fail to notice. I had often wanted to put my arms around her and be close to her, but never since the day of my return had I ever broken down that cold reserve that had grown up between us. Nevertheless, I was surprised to see Mum in that green silk dress, and more surprised when she announced her intention of taking a walk as far as the lane and Fry's Farm. She applied some lipstick as she passed the mirror on the wall in a slightly amateur way, and when she looked up I was shocked that the colour was too harsh for her and she had gone too high on the lip contour which gave her a clownish look. I said nothing, but later that afternoon, as I was returning from the shops through Halls Road and down into the lane, I was positive that I saw a glimpse of green silk dress just behind the pavilion of the tennis courts at the top of the lane there. I had misgivings, and hurried home as fast as could.

25 · *An Experience*

Just before you turned the corner into Waters Lane where the packing department of Langridge's stood, there were five stone steps leading up to the Tizer factory. Aerated mineral water had just descended on us in Kingswood, and the firm was going great guns. For weeks now, white-coated salesmen had been knocking on every door in the street with crates of fizzy lemonade in different flavours, offering one bottle free for every three bottles sold. The firm had taken over the premises at the top of Waters Road and the word TIZER was emblazoned over the door. Every morning we rounded the corner for work, all the young lads would be huddled outside waiting for the door to open to admit them to start work. There was always plenty of wolf-whistling and cat-calls from the lads as we passed. As I came up to the corner one morning, a young lad was pushed into me by his companions who shouted out,

'Hey, Miss Dropcurls, this young fella likes you!'

When we had both regained our balance, I gave him an angry look, tossed my head and proceeded haughtily on my way. He looked haunted and gave a quick look towards the lads who were making ridiculous noises and urging him on. I was embarrassed, especially when in some kind of desperation he shot his hand out and grabbed me by the arm.

'Let go,' I shouted at him, 'Let go!'

I was aware of several of my workmates who had now come on the scene and they joined in on my side whilst the lads shouted encouragement on his.

'See me tonight,' he blurted out, 'Please?'

It was fairly obvious that the other lads had dared him to make this date after expressing a liking for me, and I thought that by agreeing to meet him it would satisfy the lads, I could proceed on to work and that would be the end of the matter. I had to suffer the good-natured backchat of the girls, but by the time dinner time came round, I had forgotten all about the incident.

At six o'clock that night, just as I stepped out onto the street to go home, a small figure appeared beside me and took my arm.

'Oh no,' I yelled at him, 'Not you again!'

'Will you come to my house for tea on Sunday?' he urged, 'Say yes, I want you to say yes. Please say you'll come.'

We reached the corner and he ran forward to jump on the tram. 'I'll tell my Mother to expect you.' he called out as the tram shuddered and clanked on the lines and the overhead cable flashed a blue spark as it gathered speed.

The next day he was there again, very confidently stepping out of the line of lads and actually taking my arm started to walk me to the door of the packing department. I shook my arm free and asked him what sort of game he was playing. He wasn't any taller than I was, but he had the most beautiful mouth I had ever seen and the whitest teeth when he smiled. His eyes were deep brown with fringes of long lashes. He was small and beautiful. He said his name was Bert Harris and there on the steps of the Tizer factory, he stated his intention to marry me. I opened my mouth in amazement and then laughed with scorn. Looking back on that incredible first romance, I know now that I could have fared a great deal worse.

'Sunday?' he called out after me — and, 'I'll meet you here.'

I hadn't meant to go, but the sun was bright and shining and a natural curiosity prompted me. Besides, I thought, I owe him that, especially as the lads had almost pushed him into it. He would be made to feel terrible if I ignored the date he had plucked up so much courage to make. He was there on the steps waiting. A look of relief passed over his face and the white teeth grinned and his small stature drew up another inch as he swaggered over to me and possessively took my arm. I primly withdrew mine from his. I felt hurried, as though events were moving out of my control, and I was certainly not going to allow that. At the same time, I also felt that the action harnessed me as though I was now his property and I wanted the wild freedom of my own choice. We began to walk down the main road and several times he took my hand and held it lightly. And as many times I disengaged it and finally stuffed both hands into my pockets. Still, as we walked along he kept peering at me with his bold dark eyes and I was disconcerted and looked straight ahead.

When we neared Plummers Hill which was almost into St. George where my grandparents lived, he made a quick turn to go down over the hill. Just inside, and lying back from the hill were three cottages with long, pretty gardens. The flat wooden front door had a huge black knob on the side which opened the door to reveal a large square flagstoned room which comprised both living room and kitchen. A flight of stairs ran parallel with the far wall, with a greasy black bannister rail extending from the bottom to the top. The black panelled board beneath the bannister gave the appearance of having had countless numbers of layers of black paint brushed on it, and great iron coat pegs in one unlovely row supported coats, trousers, hats and scarves. There were even a couple of dog leads, though I saw no sign of a dog.

Mrs. Harris was a tiny thin wisp of a woman, with thin pinched features and tiny fragile wrists. She was sitting in a dilapidated armchair nursing a finger that was bulging with layers of cotton wool and bandage. She was gently rocking herself back and forth, and at the same time, supporting her wrist with her one free hand whilst thrusting the bandaged finger out in front of her, as though she couldn't bear to have it nearer to her. Nobody took the slightest notice of her and her almost inaudible moaning was discreetly ignored. Mr. Harris was half hidden from view with his head in a cupboard and sounds of tools chinking and clanking from the interior could be plainly heard. Only his legs were visible and Bert called out loudly several times to him, before a tool was thrown down violently, accompanied by a very colourful expletive. When his head and shoulders emerged from the dark depths of the cupboard, and his eyes focused on me, he gave a wide grin and proceeded to wipe his hands on a filthy rag, and struggling to his feet, he took my hand in a warm firm grip. In fact, he kept it there and even covered it with his other free one, looking at me with the same bold audacious stare that Bert had given me, except that with Mr. Harris I experienced a strange feeling in the pit of my stomach that I did not understand and which brought a flush to my face and I felt my cheeks burn. Bert Harris was a small replica of his father. In middle age, he would be exactly like him: a very exciting, vibrant man. Yet, as I looked around that kitchen, every instinct in me was revolted at what I saw — the hallmarks of simple poverty.

From the cracked china on the dresser, to the bits of ragged covering on the flagstones it all set up such a violent reaction in me that I wanted to run and run. The image of Elsie's house, with the warm carpets and great leaping fires in all three rooms, the flowers, the velvet curtains, the warmth and well-being that money can realise flashed again in my imagination. I closed my eyes. No, I must never relinquish this picture of what I wanted in life. I could not, and would not settle for the lot that had been my Mother's. That look she often threw me I must prove to be wrong; this boy who was a bottle-washer in a lemonade factory was far from the sights I had set myself.

Mr. Harris and Bert got the tea and finally removed Mrs. Harris from the scene. Mr. Harris helped his wife upstairs with the offending finger still rigidly in front of her. I learned at the tea-table that she had a whitlow.

'She just needs it lanced.'

Mr. Harris said this as though he could just as easily

have done it himself with his toolkit if only the stupid woman had allowed him. I was glad to leave, but with more winks and nudges than I thought necessary he finally touched my hair admiringly and leaned forward to kiss me. Again, I experienced a thrill like a ripple that ran through me. When I looked at Bert, he too was smiling with pleasure. It was as though they had captured something that gave pleasure to them both. On an impluse, I suddenly saw a tramcar stop at the top of the hill, and began to run as I waved them goodbye. I called out, 'See you tomorrow, Bert.'

And caught the startled look in their eyes. I hoped I never would.

In the days that followed, I skilfully avoided Master Harris. Whilst he waited at one door, I escaped through another. Sometimes it meant enlisting the help of mates. We giggled uncontrollably when a note was passed to him explaining I would be working late, and whilst I was escaping through a window at the back of the building, Bert apparently settled himself down to wait. One night, he anticipated what I was doing and worked out the layout of the warehouse. He was waiting for me as I emerged from weeds and nettles into the lane.

'Run!' my workmates called with glee, 'We'll hold him off.'

They did, but not for long. Bert was small, but strong. He caught up with me breathless and panting, and pinioned my hands against a wall. He was very angry that I had made a fool of him. We just stood there looking at each other. I couldn't say anything because of the hurt look in those brown eyes.

'You don't like me as I like you,' he said at last.

'No,' I said simply and let it go at that. How could I tell him the real reason?

'I love you,' he went on, but his voice was flat. Then — 'My Father thought you were lovely too.'

'I'm sorry,' I said gently, 'I truly am.'

He let go of my hands then and began to walk slowly

116

away, but stopped short and came back and kissed me softly but firmly on my mouth. Without warning, I experienced this warm exciting tingle all over my body and I wanted to respond. Instead, I stiffened and put out my two hands to push him away. He released me and stepped back and then walked away. I felt ashamed, guilty and confused.

26 · A Holiday

The days and weeks passed and were fulfilling. To my utter joy, Vee was now working at Langridge's — although she was working a machine and on piece time rates, which didn't even give her the time to glance up from the endless stream of corsets which she fed into this great mechanical monster. We got together at weekends, and some weekdays when work was done, and enjoyed the limited leisure time that was available.

We went to the Hippodrome to see David Hanson in the musical 'The Student Prince' to hear him sing my favourite song which was (and still is) 'Golden Days'. We also enjoyed Ann Zeigler and Webster Booth.

One year we went camping at Uphill with four other girls who worked at Langridge's. My Uncle took us all down in the back of his van and we camped in a small paddock that belonged to a farmer, Mr. Pringle. Two lads, who called themselves Bill and Cody helped us to erect the heavy old canvas tent, and it was they who came to our rescue that night when we were all flooded out. Mr. Pringle made available one of his hay barns, where fresh straw had been put down for all of us. When Elsie Philips realised that we were all going to doss down together, boys and girls, she got very annoyed and said she was going straight home. Old Mr. Pringle said it was the best he could do for the moment and told the lads

Joyce in her precious coat

to be on their best behaviour and to look after the
girls. Meanwhile, in the morning, he would make other
arrangements.

Both Vee and I enjoyed the situation very much.
Blankets were thrown over makeshift lines to divide the
male section from the females, but nobody slept that
night and we sang into the early hours when Bill produced a harmonica from his jacket. Never had we been
so taken care of. In the morning, it was the lads who went
outside and lit a fire and later brought us steaming mugs
of tea. And when Mr. Pringle offered to let us take it in

turns to use his kitchen Bill and Cody offered to be the cooks and brought us plates of beans and bacon which tasted good.

We decided to be pioneers and brave out the week. It was no hardship really, the boys took care of that. The barn with its litter of clean straw was warmer and roomier than any tent, and the lads were found a shelter in a hay loft about twenty yards away. We used the kitchen and the bathroom at the farm and that holiday was a pleasant memory to look back on.

We found an old wreck of a ship half-buried in the baked mud and sand just off the shore at Uphill. Most of our time was spent on this old wreck. The lads tied me to the mast, and they were Pirates. I rather suspect that as I was the littlest girl of all of us, they found it easiest to catch and tie me up. I was sixteen then, five foot tall and weighed about six stone and a half. I could race them all up the hill to the church at the top; I could climb as well as any boy and run like the wind. Best of all, I loved to roly-poly down a hill. I longed to learn to swim, but was terrified of the water. And much to my dismay I remained as flat-chested as any lad.

But I felt and loved the wind in my hair and the freedom of not being fettered in tight restrictive clothing. I was as wild and free as the wind which whispered to me in the dying of my childhood, 'You and I are one, stay a while longer yet — not yet — not yet . . .'

When we returned to work the following Monday, I was eager to relate the events of the holiday, but Elsie Philips begged me not to tell the incident of the barn. She said that if her Father ever found out that she had spent the night with half a dozen boys in a barn, she would be thrashed within an inch of her life. It had never occurred to me that any Father would take such drastic action, although Elsie had said that her Father thought that she had spent the holiday with a married sister.

'I shall never forgive you.' she said, 'If you ever breathe

119

one word about the damned holiday and I wish I had never gone.'

I did get the impression at the time that it was not the holiday she was anxious about, but the guilt of having to tell lies in order really to enjoy herself. I was always feeling guilty about something, so knew just how she felt. So nothing was said about the holiday, but I did tell my Mother about the night of the storm, rolling about with laughter at the comic sequence of it all. My Mother's face did not move a muscle. She stared hard at me as though I was making the whole thing up. It was as though there was condemnation in her eyes. As though at sixteen I was capable of every seductive device that would bring a lad or man to my side. Like Elsie, I did not enlarge on that holiday. But unlike Elsie, I was not afraid that I would have the living daylights belted out of me. My Father had never belted or chastised me; I had had more freedom than a lot of girls but how I wished I could have talked to Mum about so many things about growing up. Instead, a look like that did more to hurt and defeat me. I think a belting would have demanded a reason; the harsh look sent me back inside myself and further and further away from Mum.

My Mother had been very quiet of late, I had even caught her crying softly as she sat at her machine. Plainly she was unhappy, but she always got up and left the room the moment it came upon her. Every day when I came home for dinner, I brought with me a new girl called Katy James. She would bring some sandwiches and would make a cup of tea. Katy sat giggling and simpering about nothing in particular, she was empty-headed and vain. She had a very round face with a lot of pimples around her chin and mouth. She had the most beautiful fringed eyelashes, that swept on to her cheeks, she fluttered them coquettishly every time she dimpled a smile. She irritated me. Katy's sister Pet, worked in Miss Golding's Haberdashery shop in Regent Street. Katy boasted of her,

'The most beautiful creature in the world, you should just see her.' I couldn't wait. Anything had to be an improvement on Miss Katy.

So, after we finished our dinner, we decided to take a stroll as far as Regent Street and I would see for myself that she was not telling lies. We ran up the lane and into Halls Road. Halls Road brought you into Regent Street and right opposite the Maypole. On the other side of the pavement was Golding's. There stood Pet, bearing a striking resemblance to her sister, with the same round moon face and large long fringed lashes. When they giggled together, it remined me of the two ugly sisters in the Cinderella Pantomime. Pet was prancing up and down giving little jumps like a cat on hot bricks, when Katy looked up and saw someone and shrieked,

'Oh Pet, he's coming, he's coming!'

I turned round and there was Patrick O'Hara wheeling his bike and grinning at the two girls who clamoured round him almost swooning, slamming their eyelashes like great fans.

Patrick did his little tap dance routine and looked pleased with all the attention he was getting. The look he gave me warned me to stay clear of the dark back way near my home. I decided that he was an outrageous lady-killer and flirt; the younger the better, in fact. Kate and Pet were having a whale of a time. Presently they would both be boasting that it was self evident that Pet was attractive, she could already draw a man. I felt slightly bored with the whole affair and said I was going to carry on walking back to work. I left them both and turned to go. As I glanced towards Halls Road I thought I saw my Mother peeping out behind the houses but I dismissed the whole idea and went on to work.

That night, my Mother was crying again and my Father was visibly upset as well. For the first time ever, I heard them having a row and finally my Mother ran upstairs and I heard her crying. My Mother was pregnant again and I heard Dad telling her he was sorry that it had happened. I felt a great wave of sickness come over me. Why was it that all the women who became pregnant always wore that totally resigned face? She hadn't wanted me or Dennis; she had no patience with Clifford now; she was not even happy with the news of this one. Why did men give women babies they didn't want? Life certainly was not simple.

27 · *Brian*

My Mother emerged the next day, with red eyes and announced that she did not want Katy to come home with me at dinner time any more. She also made a bitter attack on my behaviour outside the Maypole,

'Right there in the middle of Regent Street,' was her scathing comment, 'Three giggling females all asking for trouble, and you were the worst from what I saw and what Patrick said.'

'Well, ' I retorted angrily, 'He would have to say that, wouldn't he? He'd have to make me out to be a liar in order to establish his own innocence. And with his Irish blarney, he shouldn't find that at all difficult.'

'He doesn't like you, either.' Mum's eyes were bright and defiant, 'He says you stop him in the lane and encourage him.'

We stood facing each other and I said sadly,

'Is that what you believe, Mum?'

I didn't wait for a reply. Somehow I just knew that I would never get near to her ever, and that nothing would be the same again.

Towards the end of the year, Mum gave birth to a baby boy who she called Brian. He was a handsome little fellow with brown eyes like his Mum's, a chubby, chuckling happy little baby who my Mother adored. She cooed and crowed over him and left us to fend for ourselves. It was

Clifford who suffered the most for he was only seven and still a very nervous child and needed a lot of attention. Now the responsibility of Cliff was thrust upon me, and I often had to Mother him and pacify him to get into bed and be with him.

My Father fared no better, for it seemed as though, with the birth of Brian, my Mother became her own woman and did what she wanted to and the Devil take the rest of us. It wasn't that she refused to do the things she had always done without murmur. It was as though she had released herself, and made the rest of us do more.

Patrick O'Hara vanished from our lives as quickly as he had come into them. He had a reputation with every young girl in Kingswood. Finally, a school-mistress caught and captured and married him. She was a quiet, demure little mouse of a thing, who one would think couldn't say boo to a goose. But teachers have to know how to control a class of unruly youngsters if they are worth their salt and I think she knew just how to control Patrick. At any rate, he suddenly disappeared from the High Street altogether and settled down in quiet retirement somewhere in the country.

Meanwhile, Mother and son joined forces and ruled our household. He could do no wrong and as the days passed I felt a growing awareness that even my presence was superfluous and I felt sad, lonely and afraid.

Saturday was the day that all the brass had to be cleaned. That was my job. Dad had the whole house filled with brass ornaments that he had lovingly brought home for my Mum. There were candle holders and brass crosses of all sizes. Horse brasses and ashtrays. The companion set in the grate was brass and the great brass fender had been bought to match. Even the lion head knocker was brass. The handles on the doors were brass, below brass finger-plates and over the front door was a sheet of brass that had to be continually cleaned. Two solid brass horses each side of the mantelshelf were a

work of art, and the pride and joy of my Father, but the bane of my life to me. It took a whole of a morning to complete the task of cleaning and I along with my mother, hated it. I merely loathed the task itself; my Mother hated the ornaments. There came a time when she warned Dad not to bring another single brass thing into the house. Pointing to the brass horses over the mantelshelf she said,

'They must weigh half a ton. If they fell on anybody's head he'd be pulverised!'

Dad looked at the two rearing horses, with a young lad pulling at the reins with pride and then began to sing quietly. This only served to enrage Mum further and she would burst forth in angry protest,

'D'you hear what I'm saying, Chas? I want no more of the bloody stuff in my house!'

In the weeks that followed, I noticed when I was cleaning the brass, that several little items were missing. I said nothing for a very simple reason: if they weren't there, I had less to clean, and my task would be finished all the earlier. However, something happened one Saturday morning that shocked me and made me feel very sad.

The ash bins were collected every Saturday, and in those days, the men actually opened the back gate and walked up the paths to collect them. They wore some kind of leather harness over their shoulders and down one side of them. They would skilfully twist and hurl the bulging bin onto a shoulder and walk with it down the path and into the lane, where with one more twist of dexterity, they tipped the contents into the waiting lorry. They would then return the bin to its rightful place and replace the lid as well. As a final gesture, if the woman of the house was anywhere around, the dustman would doff his cap and quietly close the gate behind him. Ashbin day was an exciting interruption from the norm.

Joyce's Mum and brother Cliff

This morning, my Mother was standing very silently behind the curtain in the sitting room. Periodically, she peeped out where she had an uninterrupted view of the garden path right down to the gate. When I came into the room she made a sign for me to stay quiet and to get away from the window where I might be seen. I sat on the box fender and looked puzzled. I did not have long to wait for events that followed quickly. The young man from the Corporation made his way up the path, and without looking inside the bin removed the lid and went to hoist it up on his shoulders. When he found that this familiar and simple task was impossible and that he had nearly done himself a nasty, a look of sheer surprise came over his face. At this point, my Mother was bent almost double with suppressed amusement. Meanwhile, the young man had found out the reason for the rigid immobility of the bin and the look of surprise had now given way to a lot of sly and furtive eye-darting — up and down the path and in all directions. Finally, when he established that not a soul was about, he whistled to his mate who came to his side and for a few seconds engaged him in low conversation. The two of them advanced cautiously up the path again and stood looking into the depths of the bin, then looking at each other as though they couldn't believe the evidence of their own eyes. Then, they both took a handle on either side of the bin and together they carted it triumphantly away.

All this time, my Mother was almost choking with uncontrolled amusement. She hung on to the side of the table and shook with laughter. I looked on in grim shocked silence, for I knew that half the precious items that Dad had so lovingly crafted for her had now gone from the house and were now the dustman's perks.

'Mum, ' I said, 'How could you? Dad made every one of those things for you!'

Her face and mouth hardened and she almost spat out at me, 'I hated every one of them. And now you won't need to moan and groan because your precious Saturday is disrupted.'

Before five years were out, there would be a war. Nobody knew it then, but I often wonder, when the price of brass rose to a staggering figure, whether she ever looked back on that incident and would ever be ashamed enough to admit that the final laugh was on her.

28 · *Reunion With Dennis*

At seventeen, Vee was courting. I was devastated. Everything seemed to change overnight. Now there would be no more cosy evening chats and weekend jaunts to the cinema.

'Vee,' I said, 'You must be mad.'

'I love him,' she replied, in a tone of total conviction.

'What utter rubbish,' I shouted at her, 'How can you possibly know all that in five minutes?'

I was utterly devastated and dejected. I hated Cecil Garland. I hadn't met him, but if I could have eliminated him I would have done. Vee was my best friend, and for the first time in all those cosy years someone had come between us and it could never be the same again.

'Be happy for me,' she said, and put her hand on my arm. 'What would have happened if it had been you instead of me?'

'Oh Vee . . . 'I said and clung to her and cried.

Cecil Garland was a dish. He was blonde with blue eyes and worked on the buildings. That night I went to Morris's school of dancing by myself, although we had both of us arranged to go. I thought that if I now had to do things on my own, I might as well hurry up and get on with it. I had a new pink taffeta dress and a deeper maroon bow for my hair, and a black velvet cape. I felt and looked good. If only I could have developed a bosom, I would have had all the confidence in the world. Morris's school of dancing was in Deighton Square and I had to catch the tram to get there. My first impression was that the hall was filled with potted palms, and doorways hung with long strings of coloured glass beads which made a swishing sound as you passed through. And the coloured lamps in the shape of lanterns gave the hall a faintly oriental look. There was a three-piece band consisting of a drummer, pianist and saxophonist. I was surprised to see that the drummer was my brother, Dennis, who immediately came down from the raised platform to welcome me warmly, and continued to talk in the interval and again at the end of the evening. We were pleased to see each other. He introduced me to his friend, Roy Coombes, who played the saxophone.

Roy was a slightly built young man with a pale unhealthy pallor. He didn't look at all strong to me. He had serious, deep set eyes and a moustache. We found a lot to talk about and I suddenly found myself laughing easily with the both of them. Dennis now had a sense of humour that matched my own, and at times we laughed uncontrollably about little instances that had happened in our family way back in the dark past. He was interested to know about Mum and Dad, and was surprised to know he had another brother. He said he was now a conductor on the buses, but played with Roy sometimes in the band for the Saturday dances. I asked him about Ada and Frank and then he was serious when he spoke about her. He lowered his voice a little to tell me she was having some kind of treatment for depression.

'Frank and I have to do everything for ourselves,' he confided. 'That's not exactly what he had in mind, was it?' I said.

It was evident that he wanted to be loyal, but also plain that things were not as they should be.

'She often talks about you,' he said at length. He bent

Joyce with big brother Den

128

lower and smiled confidentially. 'You know Jayce' she says, 'I wish I was like Jayce, she ain't scared of nothing. She's strong, she'll always get by.'

'I have bravado,' I mused, 'But I'm not brave.'

Roy Coombes called me 'Little Joycee' and offered to run me home on his motor bike. I urged Dennis to make time to come and see Mum and had a mental image of Ma Saunders assuring her that the fortune teller was right after all, and that Denny had returned to the fold. As I flung my arms around my brother to wish him goodnight, I could see Ma Saunders wiping her hands on that coarse brown apron and pushing her ragged old cap further over her wispy, wayward hair saying,

'Dost know, Nell, I da mind the time when my Old Aunt did go to that Old Rhoda womun to get the tea cups read. There, they don't hold with it, but I swear she got the knack all right. Now, take my old man (that is, if you want to) . . .' and here she would cackle, nudge my mother and almost knock her over, 'Well, now he da think it's a lot of dangerous nonsense but I bet he wouldn't take a walk on a dark night down as far as Sally on the Barn.'

Dennis promised to visit my Mother and I got on the back of Roy's bike and we roared off with the biting November wind stinging icily into my face. I shivered and pushed my face further into the back of his coat and clung tighter around his waist with my two hands. After that, he called for me regularly every Saturday. Dennis kept his promise and had a tearful reunion with my Mother, although he never did come back home to live; and Mum was too taken up with the new baby to grieve for long. She said that to cry for a whole day and a night was long enough to howl over anything, and that while she was howling over other people, they were not howling over her. She directed this piece of logic at me, but I know if I had asked her whether she meant me or not, she would have concluded the conversation with the classic remark,

'If the cap fits, wear it, girl.'

On Saturday when Roy came to pick me up, his bike coming to a shuddering halt outside the house, she saw me all dressed and waiting and cryptically remarked,

'Your boyfriend's here on his flying bedstead. If you land up in a field tonight, don't leave the gate open — you might catch cold.' Ma Saunders would have been much more blunt and to the point. She would have retrieved a hairpin from beneath her old man's cap and poking it in her ear to give it a good scratch and pick out the grot, would have asked me outright,

'Is 'e the fourth or the fifth?'

On Saturday nights, just as I was ready and about to go out, Dad would raise anxious eyes in my direction, tell me to be a good girl and not to let him down. I used to think that he meant that I must always be nicely dressed and not look common. I always brushed my shoes giving them an extra brush around the back, and made sure that my coat length was the same as my dress. I always stood in front of him and asked if I would do. My Mother would smirk and Dad would cough and go outside. Mum would then say,

'Now don't be late back, and no mischief, my girl — you know what yer Father means.'

It was some time before I found out. That was the night I had gone to visit Katy Jones who was now married and had a baby and was living in rooms in her parents' house. As I left, my Mother's only comment had been a pronounced sniff.

My way necessitated negotiating a dark, but gas-lit alleyway, and tripping along brightly I had only been dimly aware of a man in a light raincoat coming up behind me. Danger signals had flashed into my head too late to prevent the man from suddenly lunging at me and pushing me against the wall, where his great wrist and hand disappeared up my clothes and into my knickers. The shock was electrifying and I felt violated and very angry. The anger burst forth almost immediately and I tried the same tactics on him that I used on the enemy who was Ma Saunders when she tried to stop me climbing The Mountain. I screamed as loud as I could into his ear, which wasn't difficult because what he had in mind made it very necessary that he stayed extremely close to me. With his ear drum obviously shattered, he took a step backward so quickly that my knicker elastic slapped my leg with a whack that made me wince, and I began to bash him about the head with my handbag. He put both hands over his head to protect himself and began to back away.

'How DARE you, ' I heard myself saying, 'How dare you even touch me. My Father will kill you. He won't like it at all!'

Several people arrived on the scene at that moment and the man in the grubby raincoat vanished into the night and only then did the anger subside and I was left white and shaken.

That was the night, I learned that whatever my Father wouldn't have liked, I didn't bloody well like it either. The more I learned about sex, the less I understood it. When I finally related the incident to my Mother, she told me without hesitation,

'You should have had more sense than to go through the alleyway at all at that time of night. I thought you would have had more sense.'

Well I couldn't win, could I? From that moment on I became very, very alert in dark shadowy places and made damn sure it wouldn't be my fault next time. I sometimes wondered if the old ancient wisdom was the lesson that I learned so painfully.

29 · *The Giant Slobberer*

I remember another incident late one Saturday night — very amusing in retrospect, not so funny at the time. I hadn't really enjoyed the dance that night. Some of the lads who were the good dancers hadn't turned up, and the remaining few were either very ham fisted, or fell over their feet and trod on your toes. I found myself yanking them round corners whilst they still counted out the steps. My feet were sore and my hands were sticky. I suddenly smelled the dust on the floor and became aware of the bizarre artificiality of the whole set-up. I felt tired and depressed and more than ready to leave for home. I did not want to wait for Roy so when his friend Bob offered me a lift home on his bike, I accepted with alacrity.

I was glad to climb up behind him on the big Norton, and he patted my bottom lightly to assure me that he was about to be off now that he knew I was safely aboard. I didn't look at the road ahead as the road was too keen, and in ten minutes I knew that I would be home and safely tucked up in bed. We had been moving for quite some time before I realised that the sounds of the main road traffic were not in evidence and everthing was quiet all around us except the steady drone of the motor bike. I dimly recognised Trooper's Hill and the country road leading to the river and Sally on the Barn, a familiar beauty spot in the Summer, but reputed to be haunted.

'Hey,' I yelled out, 'What's going on?'

'Got to stop a minute, Joyce, Baby's playing up, ' Bob said, just a shade too glibly for my liking.

'Baby' was propped up against a wall and Bob removed gloves and fiddled with spark plugs.

'Shan't be a minute,' he called out, and then led me off the road and sat me on a wall on the far side of the road where I swore softly under my breath and my teeth chattered with the cold.

'Why did we have to come all this way?' I yelled to him across the road.

'All will be revealed,' he called back, 'In just a tic.'

It was.

He came swaggering over and put his arms around me.

133

'Cold little Joyce, ' he crooned, 'I shall stop the chattering of those tiny teeth.'

Those tiny teeth would have loved to have turned into fangs and buried themselves into his silly neck except that he was muffled up to the ears in motor bike gear. What happened next will remain a permanent fixture of my horror scenes for the rest of my life. As he opened his mouth to kiss me, I noticed that he didn't have a tooth in his head. He placed the whole of his toothless mouth over mine and proceeded to wash my face and scrub my chin all the while making the most revolting sucking and slurping noises possible. I gathered strength and wits and loins together and with one mighty yell I pushed him reeling over backwards and into the muddy gully beneath the wall. I reckoned I'd had enough of sin, sex and seduction to last me the rest of my life. I scrubbed my face with my handkerchief and quickly hopped down from the wall where the cold stones were not doing a great deal for my backside or my comfort and watched in horror as Bob, with the last remnant of his pride (which, let's be fair, had been badly sandpapered), walked slowly to the bike, adjusted the strap on his helmet, slipped on his gloves, kicked the bike into life and sped off down the lane.

That left me alone with the wind sighing dismally in the trees and my heart thumping like a drum. All of six miles from home. No time to sit and dwell on ghosties and things that go bump in the night, or wonder what to do if the grey figure of Sally met me on the road that night. So I started walking. Every time the wind blew through my coat I shivered. It seemed to penetrate right through to the thin dance dress underneath. I began to dream about hugging a hot-water bottle and snuggling down underneath the blankets and the big eiderdown on top. I was still a long way from home. It would be the early hours of the morning before I got home, and I doubted if anyone would believe the story of the giant slobberer. 'The giant slobberer strikes again!' I suddenly thought and started to laugh to myself, but had to stop because the laughing and the cold made me want to spend a penny. I was just debating whether I should risk stopping behind one of the great oak trees along the road, but decided that I couldn't take the chance. It was the haunted bit of road and I didn't want to get caught with my pants down.

It was then that I heard the sound of a motor bike coming towards me, and the next moment Bob had stopped by the side of the road and with a curt 'Get on' stayed long enough, with his legs straddled either side to balance the bike. I needed no second bidding and hopped aboard real smartish, and we sped towards Kingswood and home. I breathed a sigh of relief and wondered if I could manoeuvre the stairs to avoid the ones that creaked so that my Mother wouldn't know what time I'd eventually come in.

I hardly glanced at Bob when he left me at the top of the road. I'd asked him to do this, so that the noise of the bike would not rouse Mum or the neighbours.

Next morning, Mum raised her eyebrows when she saw all the mud on my coat and dress. Driven on by some devilish gleam of mischief, for in the morning I saw the funny side of it, I related the story of the giant slobberer and to my utter amazement, I had my mother doubled up as well.

Roy Coombes did not call for me again. I began to feel there was something wrong with me.

30 · *A Pen-Friend*

It was on a warm August morning that I ran down the lane, skidded round the corner into Waters Road and into the building and up the stairs to the packing department, breathless but with a few minutes to spare before starting time. I found the Overlookers and the Pressers sitting around all engaged in happy and light-hearted chatter, leaning over the table all gazing intently at something very bright and colourful and making little gasps of wonder and delight.

Barbara Webster was a quiet, friendly enough girl who employed a limited and monosyllabic form of conversation. She had been courting a soldier who was stationed in India, for the past eighteen months, and from time to time he would send her small trinkets which she displayed to the other girls with obvious pride. I moved over the section, my curiosity aroused at this tantalizing display of the exotic colours peeping from the parcel, and leaning over the shoulders of two girls with their head bent almost onto the table where the parcel lay, was intrigued to discover that four exquisite silk handkerchiefs were displayed in rich splendour along the shiny surface of the table.

'Oh how lovely!' I burst out, 'Did your boyfriend send you these?'

'Yeeeaaa' was her only comment, but she was obviously delighted at the interest in the attention her gift provoked. 'He ain't my boyfriend 'ee's my chap.'

This added information from someone who never gave very much away, sent a buzz of interest around the group clustered round her, and eager voices now demanded to know how long this had been going on. Very shyly, she produced a small ring box and displayed a solitaire diamond ring, waving it around with the smug look of someone who had finally acquired a ring and a man. Her chap, she then informed us all, in rapt admiration at the sparkling piece of rock, had sent her the ring the' week before. The ring, she went on, was a bit too large, but the man at the jewellers had made it fit by putting a small metal clip inside it.

'Was your young man in the Army when you met him?' I asked suddenly.

'Yeeeaaa,' she answered in her usual, irritating monosyllabic way. I looked slightly puzzled, for if he was in the Army and still in India I couldn't see how she could have met him.

'I wrote to 'im,' she volunteered, 'A friend of mine who already had a chap in India sent out my address to him, and he passed it on to his mate.'

'Do you mean to say you've never even met him?' I was so shocked, that she laughed in my face.

'My friend ain't never seen 'er bloke neither, but when they both comes home on leave, we'em goin' to have a double weddin'.' I couldn't find any answer to that one. I couldn't conceive how anybody could contemplate such a foolhardy action as to get wed to a man they had never seen. It seemed the world was full of stupid females prepared to do anything rather than be left on the shelf. However, the bell broke out loud and shrill, breaking up the groups of girls who slowly dispersed and drifted to their various places. There was just barely time to whisper to Barbara,

'Well, I hope all goes well for you. Meanwhile, if there are any more handkerchiefs to be given away like those, just send my name and address to your chap and see what happens.'

I completely forgot the incident. I certainly had not meant what I said and only wished to say something complimentary about her gift and to wish her well. About a month later, a letter addressed to Miss Joyce Dark slipped through the letter box and onto the mat. It had an Indian stamp franked several times in the right hand corner. It was from a Gordon Robinson, who wrote that he was twenty one years of age, five foot ten with grey eyes and dark brown hair. My address had been passed on to him by a mate of his and he would appreciate a letter from home, and any items of news that I cared to tell him about. He said he would like a photograph and in return he would send one of himself to me.

I thought about it for a long time and then decided

that writing letters in the long winter evenings to come might be a good hobby. He could be a pen-friend, no more and no less. Just a pen-friend and I would have something to say to Barbara the very next day. I suddenly remembered the silk handkerchiefs and wondered, if I played my cards right, I might get some of them too. I wasn't so sure about the ring that didn't quite fit; and of course I must never forget the picture in my mind that now went everywhere before me — the carpets and the red velvet curtains, the solid security that only money could buy. I would settle for nothing less.

I pushed the letter behind the clock on the mantel-shelf. I would reply, but not tonight for that evening I had something better to do . . .

33 · *Sailing Too Close to the Wind*

It had rained heavily all weekend, so that as I set out for work on Monday morning, the roads were still wet and shiny. Hunched figures on bicycles flashed past me, the tyres making a swooshing sound on the rain-soaked road and the black rain capes of the huddled forms gripping the handle-bars spread out like phantom bats as they sped by.

I crossed the road at Fears the Bakers and joined a queue already forming there. From the interior, there came the most delicious smell of fresh bread and cakes. On Mondays and Fridays, they sold jam and cream doughnuts, and it was on those days without fail, that I shuffled along the line of people all waiting for these buns, and eagerly exchanged two pennies for one cream and one jam doughnut. My two doughnuts disappeared into the white paper bag. As I hurried on to work, I could feel them still warm as I clutched the corners of the bag, and I had to resist the temptation of sliding my fingers into that interior and extracting the sugar-covered doughy sweetness, sinking my teeth into the red raspberry jam until it trickled down my chin. When that one was finished, there was still the cream one, and I closed my eyes with anticipation that today's lunch would be scrumptious even to the last morsel, when I would fold the corners of the bag into my mouth, and tilting back my head to an angle level with the ceiling, let the sugar from the doughnuts slide into my mouth.

I entered the warehouse and called a greeting to Mr. Blackford as bounded up the stairs two at a time, and skidded round the corner and into the packing department. These few moments before the bell rang to commence work, were friendly, cosy ones and already there was a hum of noisy chatter. Bags of doughnuts were being handed round, and the chink of coins exchanged. Those girls who couldn't get to Fears the Bakers had arranged for their friends to bring dough-nuts in for them — the fame of those hot buns was a Kingswood byword. Even Mr. Woolrich had left the lift where he had been stacking an order, and was joking with the girls and waiting for his Monday morning treat to be extricated from a shopping bag that contained at least a dozen bags, still warm, and with just a hint of the mouthwatering grease and sugar becoming visible on the white paper bag.

We all turned suddenly, when we heard noisy foot-steps on the narrow stairway, and stood in shocked silence as a rosy-cheeked and friendly girl from our section called Barbie rounded the corner screwing up her nose like the Bisto kid as she smelt the buns and came to collect hers. It was what she was wearing in her overall lapel that made us all stop in shocked silence, for she was wearing a large red rosette that people only wore on election days.

'You'd better not let Mr. Ryall see you wearing that thing,' Miss Baxter said grimly, walking away and looking troubled.

139

'Gosh!' came a chorus of other voices.

Barbie picked up her bag of doughnuts, and with a defiant toss of her head walked to her place further down the room. Meanwhile, Mr. Woolrich made a quick movement to follow her, but just at that moment Mr. Blackford banged on the lift shaft from the floor below demanding to know,

'What the hell's going on up there? Have you all gone to sleep or somethin'?'

Mr Woolrich shouted back down the shaft to him,

'Keep your shirt on!' and then proceeded to lower the lift with the order stacked in it to the floor below. He then peered into the depths of the shaft where we all heard Mr. Blackford still grumbling and shouting to a waiting carrier van,

'It isn't my bloody fault if the van decides to arrive early before any bugger has even started work.'

Even Mr. Blackford had a white paper bag delivered to him Mondays and Fridays.

Mr. Woolrich now straightened his back, and walked quickly down the rows of Packers now busy at work. He walked to where Barbie was folding Tea Rose Brassieres deftly into cellophane bags. He spoke to her firmly and quietly, and as her face reddened she suddenly capitulated when she saw us staring at her, then she took off the offending rosette and stuck it in her pocket.

Later that morning, I had occasion to work with her to get an order completed. I was curious to know what it was all about. However, Barbie kept a rigid silence and her usually smiling face was sullen and grim. She made it clear that she was not available for comment and kept a safe distance from all of us.

When break time came and we made room in the long racks behind us to sit and eat or read whilst we relaxed, I was surprised that Barbie was the first to speak and volunteer the information herself. Ella, who was a much older girl, was seated a few feet away, with her nose deep in a novel called 'The Rose of Glen Haven.' Barbie burst out with some heat tht she was not ashamed of being a Young Socialist, and she was angry that she was not allowed to wear the Party colours . She was wearing them because there was a meeting that night at the Labour Hall and she was going straight from work. I couldn't see any harm in what she was doing, and said so. After all, it seemed to me to be a matter of simple choice which party you belonged to and working people should support the party that did the best for most people.

And I was familiar with the long litany of working-class grievances. At home, my father still cherished the dream that when Labour got into power, all would be well for the working man and woman. That 1914 war had left Britain impoverished, but it had been the poor who felt the pinch. The imperialists and war-mongers had made untold wealth and the young men had died to pay for it. Part of the socialist dream was the abolition of war, and an end to the glorification of mass slaughter and the class-struggle ended with equal opportunities for all. A grand Utopia. My Mother's views were not so lofty. She was cynically convinced that there was no party that was a hundred percent for the working class. On the eve of an Election, she maintained, they'd promise you all sorts of things for your vote, but when they got in somehow it was all changed and they were never able to carry out their promises.

'It's all part and parcel of a well-organised plot,' my Father used to agree.

Barbie cut across my thoughts. 'Have you realised just how many hours a week, a month, a year, we work for old man Ryall, for a pittance?' she said. 'If we all joined a union we could demand less hours and more money.'

Ella now glanced up from her book and called down, 'On your soap-box again, Barbie?'

Barbie turned on her with eyes blazing, 'We don't all run with the hare and hunt with the hounds. You're despicable.'

141

'I know which way my bread is buttered,' Ella continued, 'And I won't stick my neck out.'

I turned to Barbie, 'Is that what your meeting is all about?' and looked from her and back to Ella, 'Do you think then, that Mr. Ryall could object to the girls joining a union?'

Ella gave me a withering and half-incredulous stare, as if I was half mad or too naive to be believed.

'Join a union in this Tory stronghold? Organise one and find out. I've worked for worse bosses and I don't intend to rock the boat.' Ella straightened up and brushed the crumbs from her skirt. Pushing her book under her bag in the rack, she proceeded to take her leave, as much as to indicate that as far as she was concerned, she had nothing more to add to this useless argument. She disappeared down the steps.

There was something familiar about her line of reasoning and I suddenly remembered the look of almost terrible resignation on my Mother's face when Dad had come home with the news that there would not be a full week's wages to put on the table that week. How men would twist their caps round in their hands with a pitiful look of complete servitude and stand in long silent lines to queue for a job or to receive a few shillings dole money. Men lived and worked in appalling conditions and the miners from South Wales had walked all through the Dean Forest and down to Bristol through Gloucester looking for work. They had even offered to work shifts undercutting the men at the Bristol Pits. Fights had broken out at the Chequers Pub on Soundwell Road and finally everybody had joined a peaceful march down to Old Market. They had chanted on the way:

'Not a penny off the pay, Not a minute on the day.'

The women of almost every house in Kingswood gave a screw of tea or cocoa to make hot drinks for them as they passed by. Even Fears the Bakers handed over a sackful of stale bread, cakes and rolls to the women to fill with anything they could spare to give the men.

My Father had marched with the miners of Speedwell down to Old Market street and there on the cobblestones encountered the mounted police, who charged them with truncheons bashing and slashing into them right, left and centre. It was a sad day and the men suffered badly. Dad staggered home with two of his mates, he had a broken nose and blood poured down his face.

'Bastards,' he said, 'They were waiting for us.'

'What do you think we as women can do that the men have attempted and failed to do?' I asked Barbie.

'Amelia Pankhurst tied herself to the railing so that women could have the vote and have a say in the running of the country,' she commented. 'Look,' she said at last, 'You must make up your own mind about it, but you can't stay on the fence for ever.'

'I'll come with you,' I said on the spur of the moment. I still wasn't sure, neither did I feel altogether happy about my decision. On the few occasions that Elsie Storey and my Father had a 'set to', Dad was the first to retreat from the battle of words that he could not cope with, and as soon as he had made an exit from the room we would view him from the middle room window with amusement, for he would suddenly become absorbed in a sickly plant struggling for existence in the square of hard clay that served as our back yard. I was more amused than interested in politics . . .

Later that night, it was still raining as I set out for the hall. The rain beat a tattoo on the top of my umbrella and trickled down the silk-covered spokes and dripped into my shoes. They in turn kicked up the rain-sodden pavements and made muddy splashes onto the back of my silk stockings which I knew would look unsightly from behind.

I was glad to arrive at the hall, which was already beginning to fill rapidly. I spotted Barbie almost immediately. She was giving out leaflets by the entrance to the hall, and looked surprised when she looked up and saw me. 'Well', she said with a wry smile, 'I was sure you wouldn't turn up, especially in this weather.'

I sat down at the back. I took off my coat and draped it over the chair. With my handkerchief, I tried to wipe a few splashes from the back of my legs. It was impossible. With a tut of annoyance, I knew I would have to wash them when I returned home that night.

The meeting was a noisy one with a lot of heckling from a crowd of youths at the back of the hall by the door. A short, stocky man with a mass of red hair and a strong Scottish accent kept urging the crowd,

'Gie the speakerrrr a chance, mun.'

Several speakers expressed in their own way that they thought it was an immoral system that extracted huge profits at the expense of the working class, and until we all had the strength of a union around us, the capitalists would go on exploiting us. SOLIDARITY was the keyword — we must all stick together. Unity is strength.

There was much thumping on the table, which made me think of Dad when he was trying to be explicit. The people cheered and clapped their hands and stamped their feet. A scuffle broke out at the back of the hall, where a woman began hitting one of the men with her handbag.

'Don't you call my old man a lazy bugger,' she shouted, 'Just you crawl along a mine shaft with your lungs full of coal dust, and see how you like it. Nobody knows, nobody knows.'

'All right, ma,' another placated, 'Times is 'ard on allon us.'

The meeting finally broke up and volunteers were called for to distribute the leaflets urging men and women to join a union. I noted that at this point, there were only a few who eventually picked up the piles of white printed slips and Barbie was one of them. I put on my damp coat, and slipped through the door. The rain had ceased and the sky was full of stars. As I turned to walk homewards gave a sigh of relief that it was all over. How wrong I was.

The next day I was a few minutes late. As I skidded round the corner of Waters Road and up the stairs, the bell had already gone and the girls at the tables were busy with their work. Miss Baxter said in mocking stern tones,

'You'll be shot at dawn.'

Ella glanced up half enquiringly, but carried on working. I suspected that she had guessed I had gone to the meeting, but I was not going to convince her that her suspicions were correct. There was a smug look on her face. As I moved past her to continue working with Barbie, I noticed the great pile of leaflets in the rack, and knew that Ella had seen them too. I thought idly how wilful and fraught with danger this action of Barbie's had been. It was like asking for trouble to bring them in after the events of yesterday. My discomfort deepened. I said to Barbie,

'What are you thinking about? Why don't you hide them or something?'

Barbie startled me by replying,

'Why should I hide them? You are going to help me distribute them outside tonight!'

'I am?' I said, with my mouth open in both fright and surprise.

'Well, aren't you?' she said, and laughed.

I looked into those roguish merry eyes, and then saw Ella's grim, disapproving face as she glanced our way, and I threw all caution to the wind. I would strike a blow for Socialism. What could anyone do to us or tell us what to do in our own free time after working hours? Why was I so scared? It had been Ella that had started it, yet when looked at her and saw that grim smile playing about her thin lips, I still wasn't sure even when I turned to Barbie and said with forced resolve,

'Oh, alright then.'

Joyce

At five to six that night, we both made our way out into the evening twilight and took up our positions. I posted myself by the door of the machine shop on the opposite side to the warehouse. Barbie stood on the pavement outside our works to catch the familiar figures of all our workmates in that building. I shivered as I waited for the

146

shrill notes of the bell. We had escaped a few minutes early in order to take up our position. It would be a little while before the first person would arrive. At last, after what seemed an eternity, one of the cutters from that department emerged from the door. He looked up in surprise to see me waiting there with a huge pile of white forms in my hand. The smile of greeting froze on his face as his eyes took in the printed message, and with an oath he screwed it up and threw it into the gutter. They were coming out now in a long steady stream, and as they did so, I would thrust a leaflet into their hands. Some turned their shoulders slightly, so that they would not be able to extend their hands and take the proferred slip of paper. Others thrust the white slip deep into pockets and glanced furtively this way and that, whilst others read what was written and half ashamed and embarrassed, let the leaflet fall to the ground and hurried on. I sensed a wave of fear that matched my own. Not many had folded the white slip and put it into their pockets with no great air of alarm. Most everbody had dropped the offending leaflet like a hot potato. It was as though a ripple of fear had passed from one to another and they had vanished silently and quickly into the night. The leaflets lay scattered and motionless in the gutter and all along the road. A sudden gust of wind brought them all to life and they were lifted into the air and carried aloft on the breeze, the paper making a fluttering flapping noise as though a silver mocking rattle escaped from them, until with a slight gasp, the wind's breath expired and the whole wave of white floaty forms sank to the ground about fifty feet along the road and a bicycle whizzed out of the factory gates, its black tyres defacing the whiteness of the forms, obliterating the words printed there, and rendering them sodden and useless in the still night air.

I awoke on Wednesday morning with an air of impending doom. As I walked slowly to work, I had a strange premonition that all was not as it should be in my world at least. As I stopped on the kerb to watch a tramcar grind past me, the driver of the car manoeuvring the controls suddenly let out an oath and threw a handful of gravel at a stray dog who had run onto the lines immediately in front of him. 'Git out of it!' he shouted, and at the same time, he released a large wire fender called a 'dog catcher'. The dog yelped and ran to the far side of the road, his tail between his legs and obviously frightened. The driver, in long black oilskins, leggings and helmet, cursed the dog again and then pulled up the heavy wire fender which had scraped along the road for several yards.

Momentarily, I had been shaken from my feeling of doom. Now, as I again turned the corner into Waters Road, my heart thumped a little and my feet dragged themselves up the dark stairs and I came into the lighted and noisy room of the packing department. Miss Baxter gave me a half-scared look and said almost at once,

'You're in trouble.'

At that moment, another pair of footsteps sounded on the stairs and Barbie's expressionless face appeared. She walked straight to the rack where her bag and personal things were stored. She picked them up, then undid the buttons of her coat overall and laid it across the table. Without another word, and looking neither to the left nor right, she passed us for the last time. Her footsteps clattered down the wooden stairway and faded away, out of our lives forever. 'She's got the sack,' someone whispered in shocked amazement. 'Instant dismissal,' Miss Baxter said and looked vaguely troubled. She suddenly remembered something, and looking directly at me she stammered,

'You're wanted in Charlie Ryall's office.'

My legs felt like lead weights, and I began to tremble violently. The time it took to descend the steps and cross the road seemed endless. As I stood outside the office door, I had a sight of the long rows of whirring monsters, the girls bent almost double with heads held low, hardly daring to raise eyes for fearing to lose a precious second.

They were on piece time rates and their eyes never left the work. They reminded me of my Mother, sitting by the window trying to earn a few shillings to help out with the money that Dad gave her. A voice called for me to 'Come in!' and I turned the handle of the door and went in with my heart in my mouth.

Mr. Ryall and his son Charlie were standing by the window. They did not immediately turn round when I entered and I stood there, shaking and white by the table that was both work bench and desk. I suspected that the turned backs and the silence was a ruse to make me feel totally cowed. It certainly succeeded. Then both turned and indicated a chair that I almost fell into, to stop the shaking limbs. They both towered over me then, which if anything, made me feel even smaller and insignificant, so that I sank lower into the chair to try to hide my misery and shame.

'Tell me,' Mr. Ryall senior said at last, 'Are you not happy working with us?'

'Oh, I am, I am!' I cried from the depths of the chair.

Emphasising my full title, Mr. Ryall continued,

'Miss Dark — we are a small family concern, employing about two hundred people from the local Kingswood area. We do our best to ensure that the working conditions are as congenial and comfortable as possible, and we adhere strictly to the wages as laid down by the Board. Sometimes we even agree to pay more than the Board suggests. Having our employees' interests always at heart, at Christmas we lay on a party — and at no mean expense, mark you — at the Berkeley Cafe in Park Street, and I am sure we have all benefitted from this relaxing and stimulating evening. On those occasions we mix happily amongst the staff and I am sure you must agree, that we try our best to make our firm one big happy family.'

He broke off here to give me time to reflect on the happy time we had that last Christmas party and I recalled miserably how Charles Ryall had danced with

149

me and I had been the envy of the packing department for weeks afterwards. Pappa Ryall leaned closer over me and his voice now held a sterner note. As he bent even closer to me, I noticed a clump of hairs inside his nostrils. He breathed heavily as though the effect of his words would hurt him more than me.

'I doubt if a union would bring about any more benefits than the ones you enjoy already,' he said, 'I'm sure you agree with me on that point, eh?' I mumbled something inaudible and wished that the interview was at an end so that I could crawl away to lick my wounds.

'However,' and he stood back as though to brace himself for the final onslaught and humiliation, 'Your colleague was a disruptive influence and I could not allow her to lead weaker minds astray. I'm afraid it was necessary to dismiss her to ensure the smooth running of this establishment.'

Now his tone was conciliatory and he moved back to the window and stood there with Charlie looking out on to the road where two carrier vans filled with corsets from his empire were being despatched to large important firms in the city.

'I have spoken to your Manager, and he tells me that you are a good worker and this little episode is out of character. In his considered opinion you were sincere but misguided, and I respect this assessment of you. I will say no more about it, although I do not, of course, expect a repetition. Now get back to your work.'

He dismissed me with a curt nod and I fumbled for the door and fled from the room. Once outside in the street, I gulped back great breaths of air until the frantic shaking stopped and I retraced my steps to the packing department. I found the rack where Barbie and I had talked about striking a blow for Socialism and I suddenly burst into tears. I couldn't believe it when Ella left her work to kneel by my side and put her arms around me.

'Oh Ella,' I wept, 'Oh Ella.'

'I know,' she said simply, 'I understand. But don't

forget, he who fights and runs away, lives to fight another day.'

'I feel so guilty, ' I said, 'It should have been me as well as Barbie who got the sack.'

Ella's face was grim and hard and she was looking somewhere beyond the window when she said in a low voice,

'They only needed one to make an example of. The other serves to remind the rest of us not to sail too close to the wind.'

We were silent for a few seconds and I caught Miss Baxter's eye and knew I must continue with my work for her look indicated that she had already overlooked too much timewasting. I stood up and squeezed Ella's arm.

'I shall never forget this moment, or Barbie,' I said simply.

'It isn't intended that you should. Or the dream of a Utopian tomorrow. They're not scared of the dream, only the reality. That's why they make it so hard.'

I began folding the Tea Rose Brassieres into their little cellophane bags. The dream I held before my eyes returned to the wall-to-wall carpets and the red velvet curtains. I had survived. I breathed a big sigh of relief.

33 · *Yer Tiz*

I was now eighteen and earning fifteen shillings a week. My Mother said it was about time I kept myself.

'After all,' she said, 'I wasn't much older than you when I had a house and two babies to keep, on not a lot more.'

It seemed as if my Mother was casting off her grown kittens and the chores she took no pleasure in. She would take Brian for rides and walks and be out all day, leaving the rest of us to fend for ourselves. During the school holidays in July and August, she even went as far as

151

Severn Beach and camped in a tent. The wide open spaces called to her. Even Dad caught the bug and would rush down to be with her at weekends. In July, there had been a downpour of rain and the cloudburst had almost washed the camp away. All the people in the camp had donned macs and wellingtons because the ground had been so mucky and the cameramen from The Evening World had rushed down there to take photographs of the scene. They captured my Mother and Brian covered in waterproofs and carrying big jugs to collect water and printed it on the front page of that day's edition. They were both laughing and the downpour didn't deter them at all. In fact, they stayed all through August and returned home determined to go again the next year. Primus stoves and sleeping bags made from army blankets and lined with flannelette sheets, enamel cups and old cutlery were continually being stored for the following year. Cliff went along under protest. He suffered from hay fever and the great outdoors was not his idea of the good life. He suffered dreadfully in the summer when the pollen count was high and the hot sun did nothing to alleviate his misery. Sometimes he would return home on the bus and would be glad to settle in the big armchair by the window, his blue eyes streaming and a little red nose that he continually had to blow.

It was one Sunday evening, when we had all congregated at Grandfer's house, and all the family had been gathered round the organ singing,

'Oh Galilee, Sweet Galilee,
Where Jesus loved so much to be.'

Grandfer had suddenly left his seat by the organ to sit in his wooden arm chair by the fire and light up his pipe. He sucked on the stem of his pipe for a few seconds, until the tobacco glowed red and then he laughed, showing his nicotine stained teeth.

'Ah,' he said, 'We decided to go down to Redcliffe Bay

Mum and Brian camping at Severn Beach

last Saturday to find out where our May and Alf had their shally.'

It had been common knowledge to all the family that for the past two and a half years Alf had been working on a sectional bungalow. Alf was like the proverbial tortoise; slow, slow but he did get there in the end. Aunt May would get frustrated but would make a joke of it if she was telling anybody about it. She now looked up at all the enquiring faces for this was news that we hadn't heard about. That it was actually finished and located at Redcliffe Bay at Portishead was something to sit up and take note of.

'Has he actually finished it?' we all said in chorus.

Auntie May laughed easily and confided to my Mother, 'You know, Nell, I never thought Alfie would ever finish it, but it's quite nice to catch the 'bus down to the Bay, especially if the weather's good.' 'Ah,' Grandfer broke in, 'We traipsed around that there field about three times before we caught sight of our May peepin' out of the winda.'

Gran, who was fanning herself with the bottom half of her pinny cut in,

'I said to Phil, "Yer tiz'

She looked timidly round the room as though she wanted to assure us all that she was telling the truth, and that was just how it had been.

'A lot of caravans and tents in that field, never saw so many. That right, Phil?'
'Grandfer ignored his wife's remark and went on to describe the field in boring detail and to inform us that the man at the bus stop had told him that the whole field was owned by Mr. Evans.

'Ah, Evans' Field is the one you have to ask for.'

Gran thought that the man had said Ebon's Field and when Grandfer hollered at her,

'Don't be so bloody wet, woman, and wash yer lugholes out!' she began again to fan herself furiously and fell silent. He then gave us a detailed description of

154

everything that was in the chalet and how they had even had prunes and custard and cake to follow for their tea. May had done them proud and the cake was his favourite, which was seedy cake.

All eyes were on May and Alf now, as everybody began asking questions and Alf was embarrassed but pleased at all the attention aimed at his work.

'I want to make a bigger one,' he surprised us all by saying, 'And I want to take it to Dawlish.'

Without hesitation and like an arrow straight to its mark, my Mother said, looking boldly at him,

'I'll give you forty quid for the one at Redcliffe Bay, just as it is. The cash will buy you the wood to start on another.'

May looked into the grate and never raised her head. She made no sign that she approved or disapproved. Alfie hesitated a second, then he blinked and took a deep breath and said, 'Done!'

Philip slapped his thigh and shouted 'Our Nell's a card, ain't she?'

Dad's eyes were dancing at my Mother's forthrightness and Gladys, who was Perce's new wife and looked as though she couldn't take a decision to save her life, looked at her husband for confirmation that what she was witnessing was indeed all true and not a joke. 'Right then,' said my Mother. And from her handbag she drew the forty pounds and counted it out on the table. Putting a rubber band around the notes she left them on the table, asking Alfie to give her a bill of sale and receipt for the amount she had paid. The sideboard drawer was rummaged through until the pad was found and handed over the heads of Gran and Gladys. Perce produced the pen, carefully unscrewing the top, then passing it to Alf in grave silence. When the paper was finally passed to my Mother she gave a great sigh of relief and kissed the white slip passionately. It was her passport to freedom. Her first great gamble had paid off. She was independent and free and any weekend she could escape to her shally on Redcliffe Bay she was gone like a bolt from the blue. She named the shally 'Yer Tiz', and pride of place must go to this little spot for Dad planted a mass of Hester Reeds in the garden by the side and all who passed it on the windy path down to the beach stopped to laugh at the expression of the Bristol accent Yer Tiz. We never did find out how Mum acquired all that cash. When asked, she would giggle and answer, 'Ask no questions, be told no lies.'

34 · *Gordon*

For a whole year I wrote to Gordon. His letters were something special; just like chats by post, or long conversations. In imagination he took me on long train journeys in India. He had this wonderful knack of being able to describe vividly places and events that he had been to and seen.

His letters were long, wonderful epistles that came in exciting thick brown envelopes marked Part One and Part Two. They plopped through the letter-box down onto the coloured stone floor with such a thwack! that made me come rushing down the stairs to collect them. Then I would bear them away upstairs with me and I'd sit for hours browsing through them. I read and re-read them. Nobody before or since has ever written a letter like Gordon did. I loved him even before I saw him or knew what he looked like. He also sent me funny little drawings of army life which made me laugh, convincing me that he had a sense of humour that matched my own. The days that I waited for those letters were full of eagerness and pleasure. Oh yes! I did get my embroidered silk handkerchiefs from India, plus a string of cheap soap-stone beads. They came accompanied by a photograph of Gord haggling with an Indian who, in his long white robes reminded me of Ghandi. Gordon was in Khaki shorts and shirt showing off a fine pair of tanned legs, I thought. He was holding the beads aloft for me to see, whilst the Indian held both hands in the air as if to extol the virtues of the beads to justify the price that Gord seemed unwilling to pay. Obviously, they must finally have compromised after haggling over the price, as the beads were now mine.

I now had also, a sketchy picture of Gord. He was about five foot ten inches in height, slim but well-built with a mop of dark hair and a pair of very presentable long legs that looked good in shorts. I grabbed all the items and rushed off to work to confer with Barbara Webster and to show off my treasures like she had done. Barbara had not as yet met 'her chap' either, but she was in the process of getting her trousseau up together. She had decided on white satin, with the bridesmaids dressed in mauve and pink. Her mother was busy making the dresses right now.

'Are you going to marry your chap?' she enquired.

'What, promise to marry a man I've never seen?' I laughed out loud because it reminded me of the stories of all the women who trailed out to the wild west to marry men they had never seen.

'I think I shall wait to see him before I take such a drastic step.' Barbara suddenly looked up at me, her eyes were big and blue and she said earnestly,

'I love my chap, I know all there is to know about him.' I thought that was a bit of a sweeping statement, but knew that it would be impossible to get past that stoic optimism, so I didn't try.

In March of the following year, Gordon wrote to say that they were all to be released on indefinite leave, the reason for which he would tell me later. He expressed the wish to drop off at Bristol, to come to see the girl who had cheered up his lonely sojourn in India. As the day of his visit grew nearer, I was in a fever of excitement. He never knew just how my heart gave a big leap when

I first saw him standing there grinning, looking big, blonde and beautiful — all tanned like an Olympian sun worshipper. I just leaned forward and took his hand,

'How do you do?' I said politely, but was aware of two grey eyes that suddenly crinkled at the corners at the formality of my greeting.

That Spring and Summer will be forever green in my memory. That was the length of time that Gord stayed with us. We rode on bikes to all the places that I loved. Instead of my Father by my side, it was now Gord. We rode to the top of Tog Hill, then free-wheeled all the way back down again with our legs off the pedals and Gord shouting 'Yippee!' in a loud voice, and the wind rushing past us and blowing our hair about our faces. We found a pub towards evening and I had my first taste of cider with cheese sandwiches and pickled eggs from a big jar on the side of the bar. I was a bit reticent about the cider at first until Gordon roared with laughter at my wry face.

'You drink and swig your Mother's home made wine from a bottle like a veteran, yet you hesitate to drink cider,' he said.

'Home made wine is different — how can you get drunk on that?' Again he would laugh at my absurd logic, shaking his head in bewildered mock severity. We laughed aloud at silly things. One day we carved our names 'Joyce and Gordon' on a big oak tree after a sharp shower of rain had sent us scurrying beneath its mighty branches for shelter. Another day, we found a stream and lay down on the bank and went to sleep. The sun burnt our faces on opposite cheeks to each other and we giggled about that. We spent hours curled up by the side of each other reading books. Gord was an avid reader like me. He sometimes leaned over to whisper to me,

'What's he doing to her now?'

This sent me into a fit of giggles and I blushed easily, but that only made him tease me more. Sometimes when Gord was absorbed in a book, I would inveigle him into taking me out somewhere. He would suddenly throw the book to one side and chase me and I would squeal with laughter when he caught me.

We went to Dawlish Warren on the train. It cost us three shillings and sixpence. I had never been any further than Weston Super Mare on a 'charrybang' trip so that when the train ran along the seven mile track right by the side of the water, I thought I had never seen anything so beautiful in my life. The sun was shining on the water, turning it to magic, breaking it up into thousands of tiny sparkling diamonds. When we returned late in the night, I stood in the corridor and watched the moon making a silver path over the same expanse of water. Gord laughed at my quaint attempt at poetic description, but held me close and kissed me.

On the Pathe Gazette news on the films, there were disturbing scenes of Hitler's Storm Troopers at the great rallies in Germany, with Hitler shouting and gesticulating beneath the swastika banners and the crowds roaring their approval. Gord said that a war was inevitable, and they had all been told to be on immediate standby. That Summer of '38 was so warm and peaceful, people were still lazing on the beaches totally and blissfully unaware that soon everything would change in an upheaval as devastating as the first wave of the Industrial Revolution.

So far, Gord had not been to see his parents. I knew that they had written to him several times about this. I knew they were upset about it. I urged him to return home to see them. In the end, Gord decided to go home the following week. We rode on our bikes for the last time to our favourite spot b the stream. We had to cross a tiny wooden bridge and as we stood looking at the water gurgling and splashing over the rocks, the words of a poem by Tennyson flashed into my mind, and I began to speak it aloud. I was surprised and delighted to hear Gord join me and we both shouted the wrds out loud, holding hands, calling into the soft breeze,

'I chatter over stony ways, in little sharps and trebles
I bubble into eddying bays, I babble on the pebbles.

159

I chatter, chatter, as I flow, to join the brimming river,
For men may come and men may go, but I go on for
ever!'

When the poem was finished, we laughed and ran to
our special spot by the side of the stream. It was right
there that I kissed Gord and held him so tight and told
him that I loved him and would go on loving him until I
died.

35 · *Gordon Goes Home*

An open case lay on Gord's bed, into which he
would throw shirts and sweaters. We flew around, trying
to find small items that had been mislaid or just plain
lost. I found socks under cushions, and ties that had
fallen in corners. I spied a sleeveless pullover under
the cat and tried to retrieve it before Gord saw it. My
suppressed laughter gave the game away and poor old
puss got a sharp flip. That scared her, and she made a
bolt for it, swearing and hissing her annoyance as she
scooted through the back door. We searched in vain for
a special pen of his. It finally turned up in my bag for I
suddenly remembered I had borrowed and not returned
it.

At last, the case was packed, the lid closed and a leather
belt tied around to make it doubly secure. A label was
written out in block capitals addressed to his home town
all the way to West Hartlepool. It seemed so far away and
remote, like part of another land.

Walking up the incline to Temple Meads station the
next day, Gord had to change the case from one hand to
another because of its bulk and weight. We didn't speak
much, now that the actual time had come for parting, for
there seemed little to say. I was far away, immersed in
my own sadness. We passed through the barrier and onto

Joyce with Gordon and his sister

the platform. There was just ten minutes to wait and ten minutes was so shockingly short a time.

The train rumbled round the corner snorting smoke and hissing to a halt after spreading its great length along the platform. Doors opened and a stream of people trailed from the carriages all making for the exit. The low buzz of conversation mingled with the calls of the porters, and the banging of luggage being piled high on trolleys. Gord found a seat and put his case on the rack, then he came and stood by the open door. He took hold of my hands and kissed me. 'Write every day, promise?'

He didn't hear my answer for I had pulled him close to me as though I never wanted to let him go. Then I heard the guard blowing the whistle and caught a glimpse of the red flag waving and a voice called,

'Stand clear of the doors!'

Just a second of silence, then the brakes released, the hush! hush! hush! hush! of steam and the train moved slowly away and Gord was waving from the open window. I moved along the platform still waving but as it gained in momentum, the great iron monster rounded the corner and Gord was lost to sight.

The platform had emptied and I felt lonely and forlorn. A sudden vision of a white gate flashed momentarily into my mind and with it a premonition that I would not see Gordon again. Just like that day when I had rushed to the white gate and my parents had deserted me. How many times had I gone to that white gate in the days that followed to see if they would be coming back to fetch me. I had even climbed that white gate and played a game on it, 'Ride a cock horse to Banbury Cross to see a fine lady upon a white horse.' Now I couldn't breathe. I found a seat and staggered onto it feeling the same mad panic that I had felt then.

'Concentrate on your breathing, come on, take a deep breath, now another. That's better, that's a good girl.' That's what they had told me to do when a frightened nurse had carried me in to matron. The pain in my chest was relaxing, but still I sat there feeling scared and afraid for it seemed that someone else who I loved and relied on was walking away from me.

Presently, I was able to walk again through the barrier. I surrendered my platform ticket and walked through and out into the bright sunshine. When I reached Bristol Bridge, I stopped to look at the swans on the river. Then it came to me in a startling moment of revelation. Nobody could ever take anything away from me; how could the memories of that perfect Spring and Summer ever be erased? Gord and I were special people; how could a love like that ever die? I had been right to choose Gord as my first love for he had given me so many things that were good. In loving Gordon, I had become a woman.

I never saw him again.

36 · *Bertie*

It would have been impossible to have survived the following months without some kind of drastic measure. Retracing my footsteps over familiar ground where Gord and I had been together filled me with the same dreadful suffocation. In the end, although I still hoped that I would hear from him, I sublimated all my feelings and drew a black curtain across the thing which hurt so much. In order to survive, I had to do it or die. Get up, go on again, the voice within me whispered — for we search so eagerly for God only to find ourselves.

I saw Barbara get married to her soldier lad. I stood on the edge of the pavement outside Kingswood Church as she came out of the door and walked towards the waiting car, and I called congratulations and threw rose petals over her. She did not have her double wedding after all, and I thought she looked heavy about the waist. She was whisked away, and did not acknowledge my cheery greeting. I thought she looked strained and anxious and she seemed to have trouble with the frothy lace of her head-dress; she was holding it tightly as she stooped to get into the car.

I turned to retrace my steps through Regent Street and as I passed the Clock Tower the smell of fish and chips was too tempting to pass up, so I took my place in the queue and paid over four pennies for a piece of fish and a penn'orth. I sprinkled it liberally with salt and vinegar, then making a hole in the paper I munched slowly and happily along the length of Halls Road down the back way to our house, until every morsel of fish was consumed and I sucked my greasy fingers with pleasure.

When I reached the house, I turned on the cold tap and drank a long draught of water, cupping it in my hands and swigging away at it. Then I splashed the water on my face and neck and rubbed myself dry with the rough roller towel which hung on the back door. My Mother called to me that Elsie wanted to see me as soon as I came in, so I made my way over to number 35 across the road. The door was open and so was the glass inner door. I called out, and a cheerful 'Come in!' sounded from the kitchen. A long form detached itself from the chair and a pair of bright blue eyes that I recognised as belonging to Bertie, smiled into my own. He stood and held my hand in an affectionate manner. He was dressed in the uniform of the Air Force, and the dull blue of his clothes made a vivid contrast to the brilliant blue of his eyes. Elsie bustled around making coffee and twittering away that she knew how much I would like to see Bertie who was on leave and would be flying out to Ceylon any day now. It was Bertie's birthday and they had given him a watch because he was twenty-one. Almost as though this was a cue, Bertie extended his wrist to show me the watch, which he said, was shockproof and waterproof. I opened my eyes wide with approval and made suitable clucking sounds to show I was impressed. Meanwhilst, I noticed how he'd grown since I had last seen him so that he stood nearly six feet tall and good-looking, in that boyish way of his, in his Air Force uniform. When he asked if I would like to go with him to the pictures, I was on the point of making the excuse that I would be busy for the next night or two, when I suddenly remembered that there was a good film at the Regal that I particularly wanted to see. So I said on the spur of the moment that he could take me.

164

That night, I sat in the best seat in the Balcony, with a quarter of chocolates that I nursed in my lap and forgot all about until they began to melt and make a sticky mess. Bertie looked at me with rapt attention throughout, running his hand through my curls and whispering that he had always wanted a girl with dark, wavy hair. I was becoming increasingly annoyed at having the sequence of the film constantly interrupted and began to wish I had come on my own to see the film. I made a silent vow that I would eventually find it necessary to follow that plan if I was going to make any sense of the severed sequence of the story. I was glad when the screen curtains closed for the first performance, and we could emerge from the smoke filled atmosphere of the cinema into the cool outside air. He attempted to remove the dark chocolate cream stain from my skirt with the aid of his large white handkerchief, but without much success.

Bertie suggested a walk and tried to amuse me with his erudition. For a full hour I was treated to the details of the fuel consumption of a Cattalino aircraft, and the make and car number of every vehicle which passed us during our stroll. I was bored, tired and irritated by the time I reached home. I pulled the key from behind the letter-box where it hung on its piece of string and said rather pointedly that the walk had certainly made me tired and it wouldn't take much rocking to send me off tonight. Completely oblivious to this snub, Bertie fell up the steps in his haste to prolong what to him had been a successful venture. At ten-thirty, to him the night was still young. Optimism always was one of his strong points. His boyish charm another. But neither helped him much that night. He mentioned that he was thirsty and wasn't I going to ask him in? I answered firmly that I wanted to wash my hair and I was sure Elsie would still be up and would be delighted to get his supper. He looked disappointed but accepted the situation with good grace. Then he suddenly blurted out,

'If you married me, you would be coming to Ceylon!'

165

He cupped my face in those beautiful hands of his and kissed me very lightly. He stood away from me for a second, and then turned and walked away over the road and into Elsie's house.

I stood watching him and a picture came into my mind of warm sunny places and sun-soaked beaches where I could lie and become like a bronzed goddess. Escape from all that hurt. Run away and start again. I heard a door close and the dream faded, for my hurt was already safely buried under a black, black cloak deep inside me. And if I travelled to the ends of the earth I would take it with me as it lay forever buried there. Bertie was just a nice young man. I too went indoors and forgot all about him and Ceylon.

37 · *Widowhood*

By the time Vee was twenty-two, she had been married for five years and had three children and was a widow. After the birth of her third baby, she had been very ill. They had sent her to hospital where they performed a hysterectomy. I tried to get to see her as often as I could and was shocked at the change in her and the weight she had lost. She still lived in the little terraced house in Worcester Road. Then came the news that Cess had met with a motor bike accident and had been rushed to hospital. Coming home, he had swerved to avoid a cyclist, and come off his bike and fell, hitting his head. At first, he seemed all right, and with only a slight headache to show for his spill, he got on his motor bike and rode home. The pain in his head had become worse by then and he went to bed where he lapsed into unconsciousness. Vee sent for a doctor who rushed him to hospital but he died the next morning. Cess had been dead for several weeks before I heard the news at work and rushed over to see her.

Vee's Mother had the children for Vee was far from well still. She was almost bent double and looked like a very tired old woman. I immediately went into the kitchen to make some tea. When I returned, she was lying on the settee, but patted the place by her where she wanted me to sit. 'Vee, ' I said at last, 'How will you manage?'

'Like everybody else has to manage', she replied without hesitation but her voice held a note of defiance, 'I'll have the generous sum of twenty-six bob a week widow's pension to live on. At least I'll be able to count on getting it every week — they don't have any lay-offs or short weeks.'

'Oh Vee,' I said, lost for words of comfort and support. I leaned over and took both her hands in mine.

'After this lot got better,' she suddenly giggled and patted her stomach, 'we could have had a good sex life with no more shocks or worries.'

Then she leaned forward to pick up the empty coffee cup by my side and to whisper confidentially,

'Do you know, Joyce, there is one thing I am happy about that dreadful morning. I'm so happy he went from here for once without a row.'

I looked at her incredulously.

'We rowed about sex all the time,' she said.

I looked down at the floor. The awful doubts that had assailed me before came flooding back. And now even Vee. I wanted to ask her so many things but I knew the timing was wrong. I could hug her and tell her that I would come again soon. It was only when I was walking home that I remembered I had not told Vee about Gord.

Bertie did not fly out to Ceylon. He was still stationed at Southampton and so able to make several visits up to Bristol to visit Aunt Elsie and so pursue me. He would make a habit of walking down to the Works about five-thirty just before knocking-off time. His presence was revealed to me long before I saw him. It was like receiving news through the grapevine or smoke signals from the beacon. No tom-tom could have told me quicker than the girls at the factory.

'Your Airman Chap's downstairs waiting for you, Joyce. Bit of alright,' (this with nods of approval,) 'Got lovely blue eyes. I should hang on to him if I were you.'

It was all good-natured fun, but I was not ready yet for Bertie or anyone to rush me into a committed relationship, however friendly. I was slightly annoyed, not very sociable and certainly embarrassed when the nods and grins still carried on along the road. When we got home, Elsie was talking to my Mother. When she saw us, she gushed,

'Here's the young lovers then.' And immediately invited me to have tea with her and Bertie. I was being rushed along, and I felt angry at all this matchmaking. I resolved I would speak to her about it at the very first opportunity.

The following Sunday Bertie pleaded with me to come and visit his Mother.

'Just a flying visit,' he said, 'As I have to get back on the six ten train.'

I didn't think it would do any harm, so I consented to go. Bertie lived in Brislington, several districts away, but we walked it down through Hanham along the Netham, up Newbridge Road past the paper mill until we came to Wick Road and Sandy Park, down into Repton Road where the houses huddled together in one long terrace.

Bertie's Mother opened the door, and ushered us inside saying, 'Come on in, kid!'

She had the same piercingly blue eyes as her son, the same wide, shy smile. Her hands were large like his, as well, but years of hard work had knotted and reddened them. Years of toil had not enhanced them, and they looked slightly clownish now as she led the way into the front parlour and beckoned me to sit down.

Everything in that room had seen better days, from the faded upholstery of the chairs and couch, to the worn carpet and discoloured drapes. All wore the mark of an earlier era, of a more prosperous time of ease and plenty. This then was Minnie Alice. I had heard all about Bertie's Mother — Elsie had told endless tales about her. Her father had been a wealthy merchant in the city. He and another man called Barnard had opened up a chain of tobacconist's shops and had dealt directly with Wills the tobacco people. She had shown me photographs of Minnie with her sister in the garden of the big house at Totterdown. They wore long dresses and carried parasols. She went to a private school, driven there every day in a carriage. She was every inch a lady. While she was in the kitchen making tea, I looked at the photographs of three other members of the family in gilt frames on the mantelshelf, and Bertie told me that these were her three other children from her first marriage.

Over tea and cake, I enquired where Mr. Storey was. Bertie looked uncomfortable and embarrassed, but Minnie said directly,

'He went back to his Mammy!'

She then rummaged in a big black bag and produced a small silver box filled with snuff. She pushed her finger and thumb into the box and took a liberal pinch which she proceeded to shove up her nose. She offered me the box with an encouraging,

'Take a pinch, kid!'

I declined, but she only laughed, sneezing and rubbing her nose and wiping flecks of brown dust from the frill

169

of her white blouse. Again she dived into her massive handbag, this time to retrieve a tattered bar of Fry's Chocolate Cream. This must have lain amongst her other treasures for ages, for where the silver foil was rubbed and torn, there were little smudges of snuff and dust from the bottom of her bag.

'Have a bit,' she offered, holding out the sagging chocolate to me. I took the proffered piece in my hand rather gingerly, then burst out laughing. She was the oddest, warmest character I had ever encountered and I loved her immediately. When it was time to go, she whispered as if in confidence,

'Come again, kid, consider yourself one of the family.'

Bertie looked pleased that I had passed the test, and it wasn't until I got home that I remembered that one thing I hadn't wanted to happen, had indeed taken place. Bertie was now even more pleased and confident. I was less and less sure. Life was very complicated. Men that you loved did not love you, and those you could not work up any enthusiasm for pursued you with craft and cunning that you found hard to shake off.

'You are rushing me,' I protested that night when Bertie again pleaded,

'Come with me to Ceylon. I promise you won't regret it.'

39· *I Get Married*

The letter that I wrote to Bertie terminating our friendship caused such a stir and commotion, that I retreated feeling very battered, guilty and defeated.

'My darling boy is devastated!' came a wail of anguish from Minnie Alice.

She made a special visit over to see Elsie and together they commiserated. Elsie stormed over to our house demanding to know what I had done to a dear nephew of hers, who was so sensitive that god knows what he might be tempted to do. He might, she suggested, even throw himself in the river. My Mother said archly that if she'd taken notice of the times that Dad had used the same threat on her, she would be a mental wreck.

'Did he actually go, then?' I asked with incredulity.

My Mother raised her eyes to heaven.

'God!' She replied caustically, 'He'd only be gone ten minutes, then he'd be back cold as a frog, and snuggling into my back asking me to move up a bit so he could have more room in the bed.' I crossed the road to face the Storey clan once more.

'On his next leave I'll speak to him myself,' I said. I would promise nothing more for I refused to be emotionally bullied further.

My Mother thought that if Bertie were wet at all, it would be from the inside of a pub rather than a dipping in the river. Dad refused to comment and considered it to be a decision best left for me to work out and decide. I felt there were too many pressures building up for me to make a rational and calm decision.

However, I did not see Bertie for a few weeks. He did not seem too shattered or devastated. He took very coolly my decision to keep the relationship on a friendly basis and commented quietly that he was happy to know that there was still some kind of relationship at all. He said he thought that things in Europe were not good. Hitler had not kept his word and had marched into Poland; Bertie thought that war was certain. The offer to come to Ceylon was still open to me. I was to think about it and to let him know.

People were now signing petitions in the street protesting that England should not intervene in a European war and an uneasy feeling of change prevailed My Mother was unsettled too; she would often talk of selling up and going into business. I got the impression that she would be glad if I were living my own independent existence

171

Bertie and Joyce on their wedding day

away from the family, so that I too, felt a pull towards a change. As much as I hated and kicked against it, I knew for certain that the time would come when I would have to make a decision. All my life I have hated having to make snap decisions. It feels so much like a leap in the dark and brings back all those feelings of suffocation and terror.

If only I had been able to see the choices! If only it had occured to me that there were choices! If only my parents had counselled me, or shown me the alternatives! I can still feel anger that there seemed to be no concern or interest in my future welfare. I needed only a parental hand on my shoulder to direct me away from the path that even then, I knew, I should not have taken. But the only escape seemed to be in going to Ceylon with Bertie. It was time for me to leave home. The only way to leave home was through marriage. Two months later, when war was declared, young single girls across the country rushed to join the services. How I envied them! How I wished I could have gone. My life would have been full and exciting; I could have learned new skills and become a different person. The possibilities were endless. It was not to be. I had already made my choice and was married on the twenty third of July which was my twenty-second birthday.

I was awakened early one morning by the sound of gravel being thrown at my window pane. Rushing to the window, I saw Bertie down below waving a piece of paper. I opened the window and he yelled up at me that we could get married that day as he had acquired a Special Licence and the Reverend Cousins would marry us at two o'clock. I was not elated, but came down to let him in and to wait for Mum and Dad to get up before breaking the news to them. Mum's only comment was,
'I hope you know what you're doing, my girl.'
My Father didn't even glance my way, only enquiring from my Mother if his best shirt was ready for wearing. I went up to my bedroom to search through my wardrobe for something special to wear. The choice was easy, for I had only one navy two-piece which I kept for high days and holidays, so I wore the skirt with the bolero and a blouse covered with pink rose buds. Navy shoes and white gloves completed my outfit.
We all walked up the lane together, Dad in front with Bertie and Mum and I behind. There was little conversation, except that I was informed at the very last moment, after the service, that Bertie would have to get straight back on the tram and head back to Calshott. He was already Absent Without Leave and would have to do 'Jankers' — whatever that was.
It was a strange day. And a strange feeling; and not at all how I had imagined my wedding day would be. No

173

bridal dress and no friends. We reached the church door where the vicar was waiting for us in his white surplice with a gold-fringed ribbon around his neck. He held a black prayer book and smiled a welcome, looked at his watch and then waved with his book for us to follow him.

'Dearly beloved, we are gathered here in the sight of God and this congregation . . .'

I felt a sense of loss and loneliness for two people only were seated there in the front pew on this great venture into a new part of my life. I felt cold and I shivered and remembered how I had experienced the same feeling of aloneness that day I had left school with just a brown envelope containing a few inadequate words about me by somebody who didn't know me at all. There had been no handshake then, no good wishes.

Here I go again, I thought. The ring was on the book and I vaguely remember my Father stepping away from me. The gold band was on my finger now and the gold-fringed ribbon was loosely and symbolically tied around our wrists.

'Those whom God hath joined together, let no man put asunder.'

From somewhere deep inside of me, I heard a door bang shut. No escape now. For better or worse, we were man and wife. I closed my eyes and felt Bertie kiss me. There was no wild, exalting Wedding March, only phantom listeners as we turned aside to sign the Register. Joyce Dark, Spinster of this Parish, Corset Packer and Bertram John Storey of the Royal Air Force. I saw the open doorway and the sun shining outside. As we made our way to the door, my footsteps echoed hollowly all the way down the aisle.

Also of interest from Virago

JOYCE'S WAR
by Joyce Storey

'Grimsby – where on earth was Grimsby? As far as I knew, it was somewhere "up North", on the cold east coast. I had but two gifts to start me on my way, the woollen blankets from my Mum and Dad, and a half tea service from Elsie and Bert. My transition from maid to married woman had begun.'

With an army husband rarely on leave, Joyce, the mother of two girls, fights her own battles on the homefront – with air raids, in-laws, machine work and poverty – searching always for her dream house and a life to call her own.

Joyce's War is the sequel to *Our Joyce*.

THEY TIED A LABEL ON MY COAT
by Hilda Hollingsworth

'[This] passionately lived book is wonderfully evocative of its time, funny and sad . . . written from the courage of the soul' – Dirk Bogarde

Hilda Hollingsworth was just one of thousands of evacuee children to leave London at the beginning of the war in 1940. Her brilliant evocation of those childhood years – gritty, searing and rumbustious by turns – is as richly entertaining as it is heart-rending.

As the bus pulled away from the school playground, it was the last ten-year-old 'Ild and her younger sister Pat would see of their mum until the war's end. Shunted hither and yon to 'places of greater safety', their final stop was the harsh Welsh mining village where the children were picked over 'like a blooming cattle market', and where life was redeemed for 'Ild by her dauntless, loud-mouthed friend Winnie. Separated from Pat and banished to the smilingly sadistic Joneses, 'Ild was tormented by their cat and mouse games. The fire and brimstone Williams offered some solace, but next came the redoubtable Auntie Bron . . .

THE 4-VOLUME AUTOBIOGRAPHY OF KATHLEEN DAYUS

'We must be thankful that Kathleen Dayus has survived to tell her story so movingly and so well' – Jeremy Seabrook, *New Society*

'An evocation of a vanished world as vivid, moving and spiced with humour as any I have read' – Hazel Leslie, *Sunday Telegraph*

'It is a privilege to share her life' – *Good Housekeeping*

Kathleen Dayus has become a legend in her own lifetime. Born into the industrial slums of Birmingham in 1903, she left school at fourteen and started writing at the age of seventy. The indomitable spirit, humour and sheer verve that characterise her life shine out from these marvellous memoirs. Nobody has captured 'her people' with more vitality, wisdom and wit. This extraordinary autobiography – written in the splendid tradition of Flora Thompson's *Lark Rise to Candleford* and Helen Forrester's *Tuppence to Cross the Mersey* – is as evocative as any written this century.

HER PEOPLE
Winner of the J.R. Ackerley Prize for Autobiography, 1983

WHERE THERE'S LIFE

ALL MY DAYS

THE BEST OF TIMES

TRUTH, DARE OR PROMISE:
Girls Growing Up in the Fifties

Edited by Liz Heron

'Again and again, the writing calls up splendidly vivid images, audible voices, places and people that have the special, looming, close-up quality that belongs to childhood experience' – *Lorna Sage*

In this superb collection of autobiographical writing, first published in 1985, twelve women who grew into feminism in the 1970s look back on their childhoods. In feeling, circumstance, class and culture, their experiences were as diverse as they were keenly felt. But the two great landmarks in this post-war Britain of 'you never had it so good' – the Welfare State and the Education Act – were a common feature which gave to many of these girlhoods, so like and yet so unlike those of their mothers, a sense of possibility, of aspiration to a different future. These are intimate, personal memoirs, ordinary and impossible stories that remind us how individual lives are shaped in infinitely complex ways.